SAVE THE DATABASE,
SAVE THE WORLD!

SAVE THE DATABASE, SAVE THE WORLD!

JOHN B. OTTMAN, JR.

****

Interior illustrations: Lena Elkhatib

Hardback ISBN: 978-0-557-84995-6
Paperback ISBN: 978-1-4583-6368-8

The Sumo Press
350 Madison Avenue, 6th Floor
New York, NY 10017

Printed in the USA.

For Peggy

In his new book "Save The Database, Save The World!," John Ottman captures the essence of the threats we face to the information that drives business. Organized crime, underhanded competitors, and even foreign governments are looking to gain any financial, competitive, or operational advantage, and these enemies are going directly after the databases and the applications that access data. John provides a big picture view of the serious problem we face today and provides actionable steps that all enterprises, whether big or small, should be taking to protect these assets. Whether you're an IT manager or an executive who needs to understand the difference between real threats and marketing hype, this is a good resource to reach for.

Adrian Lane – Securosis

Business, technology, and threat landscapes have changed dramatically, and for the most part, our security strategies have not. John Ottman aptly draws parallels between prevailing security strategies and the ineffectiveness of the Maginot Line post World War I. Given the mainstream revelation of APTs and adaptive persistent adversaries, the stakes have never been higher. Why are they targeting the databases? That's where the data is. Defenders focus on what we manage well. Attackers focus on what we don't. While motivated adversaries will surely adapt as we better fortify our databases, available breach data clearly shows we need to better protect our data where it lives."

Joshua Corman – Research Director, Enterprise Security at The 451 Group.

John Ottman's well-written book identifies in largely jargon-free language many of the major IT security issues that businesses and organizations face today. He demonstrates that most businesses and organizations tend to focus their attentions on the perimeter while leaving their internal resources—and the sensitive data contained in their databases—largely vulnerable and unprotected. In clear and concise language, Ottman lays out a roadmap for organizations to protect their "crown jewels" from insider and outsider threats.

Mark Kagan – Government and Security Consultant

Affecting change in the manner that organizations handle database security clearly lies at the very heart of the issue when considering *practices to address today's overwhelming environment of pervasive electronic data risk. By outlining this set of concepts that help people understand how to tackle this daunting task, Ottman offers some hope as to where organizations can begin working down this path.*

Matt Hines – longtime security industry reporter and blogger

In Save The Database, Save The World!, John Ottman very effectively demonstrates the urgency of acting now to protect an asset perhaps now more precious than gold—our data. And, in this eye-opening work, it's shocking to see just how vulnerable this "gold" is to both outside and inside breaches—more than ten million databases across the globe remain largely unprotected, and 222 million records breached in the year 2009 alone. Not only does John get our attention with these vulnerabilities, but he also lays out a very effective plan of attack—or should I say counter-attack—to mitigate these risks today. Not only do organizations need to defend their data assets from outside attackers, but also from internal threats, from disaffected workers to trusted administrators that hold the keys. Organizations need to activate—and stick with—an effective security strategy that raises awareness and vigilance among all employees, and anticipates the unanticipated.

Joe McKendrick –Analyst, Unisphere Research

A well-written, comprehensive guide that every DBA, IT security analyst, and CIO/CTO should review. The book covers the key points of database security, as well as a number of obscure issues that can lead to major data breach. Save The Database, Save The World! is an excellent technical resource written in plain language.

Bob Schmeider – Americas CTO, Societe Generale

When asked why he robbed banks, Willie Sutton said "because that's where the money is". In today's reality, vaults have been replaced by databases - and criminals have set their laser sights on these valuable data stores. This book drills home the fact that with the ongoing and natural erosion (or collapse) of the network perimeter, the demand for ubiquitous data access, and the ongoing evolution of motivated, professional attackers, organizations both public and private must establish a systematic approach to securing this new perimeter - around the data store itself.

Greg Thompson, VP Enterprise Security, Scotiabank Group

TABLE OF CONTENTS

ACKNOWLEDGEMENTS

I frankly never intended to write a book about database security, risk, and compliance (SRC), but I have become increasingly passionate about the subject and wanted to share the knowledge I have learned from some very talented individuals. Writing this book has been a major undertaking, and there are many people I would like to thank for making this project come to fruition.

First, I wish to thank everyone at Application Security, Inc. (AppSec) for not only engaging with me on the mission to *Save The Database, Save The World!*, but also for helping to define our great company and the database SRC industry we lead. Since its inception, AppSec has been the first mover and the key innovator behind the rise of this exciting field. Long before I arrived here, the founders of AppSec—Eric Gonzales, Aaron Newman, and also the original CEO, Jack Hembrough—established the technology of database SRC and the business model. In the early days, AppSec's headquarters was in Eric's East Side apartment, where they spent tireless hours creating, coding, and innovating. Often waking up on the sofa after yet another late night, AppSec's founders identified the need for a solution to keep critical personal data, intellectual property, and government intelligence secure. Eric, Aaron, and Jack deserve huge credit for their pioneering roles in making the company—and the SRC sector—what it is today.

There is also a long list of contributors whom I would like to thank because they made this book possible. In alphabetical order they are: Tom Bain for editing; Rob Chapdelaine for seeing the need to write the book; John Colton for his engineering leadership; Anirban Chowdhuri and his team (especially Jayul Bhatt) for their deep knowledge of the products and solutions; Daniel (dB) Doubrovkine for his technical leadership; dB's entire development staff (too many to name) for creating DbProtect®; Lena Elkhatib for illustration; Eric Gonzales for his innovation and industry smarts; Andrew Herlands for his domain experience and editing, and also Andrew's team; Ruth Ann Holbert for looking out for us; Erik Jarlstrom for his technical skill and direction; Chris Liebert for editing; Mariya Lynch, my trusted assistant; Gretchen McMahon for photography; Dave McNamara; Ken Minihan for contributing the Foreword; Joan and John Ottman (Mom and Dad!); Jennifer Rogers for artwork development and tireless editing; Aaron Schnore for editing; Pete Schwartz for his business leadership; Josh Shaul for his technology leadership and editing on several passages; Roy G. Smith for teaching me how to write (hopefully); Thom VanHorn for establishing The Sumo Press; Richard Tsai and Mark Trinidad for content; Cecily Xi for her technical leadership, as well as Cecily's team for creating AppDetectivePro®.

Finally, I would like to thank the Metro North Railroad for providing me a quiet seat twice a day for time to write.

John B. Ottman, Jr.
January, 2011
New York City

FOREWORD

Perhaps it was the shocking clarity of the consequences of global thermo nuclear war that drove the call to action to reexamine and reestablish our strategies for national defense during the Cold War. At stake was the risk of global annihilation and the end of life as we know it on earth. Through an unprecedented collaboration between leaders from government, military, business, and academia, a framework of strategic nuclear war doctrine was created, which thus far has kept the world safe from nuclear war for over sixty years.

As the Cold War era fades, a new era of global conflict in the information age has emerged, and once again we are called to rethink the essential strategies of our national security. Strikingly, Cold War victory was achieved not through nuclear exchange or epic assaults, but rather through the deployment of a highly effective strategy of deterrence. The premise of mutually assured destruction turned conventional strategic thinking on its head. Since both sides recognized that the other possessed not only an overwhelming destructive potential, but also the certainty and resolve to retaliate after a first strike, no attack has ever been launched. While the threats and consequences of cyber conflict may be no less devastating than those faced previously, the strategies for defense must be established as the battle space is so vastly different.

Just as it was in the Cold War, technology is once again the catalyst for strategic change. The emergence of cyber space has opened a path over which an attacker can strike powerfully against our military readiness and global economy by conducting cyber attacks. The targets are our data and the systems on which they depend. In cyber war the traditional symmetries of war are upset, forcing us to reexamine the foundations of our strategic defense doctrine one more time. For one thing, conventional defense strategy requires knowing the identity of your attacker. How do we fight a war against an enemy when the fundamental principle of attribution may be in doubt?

Furthermore, should attacks emanating from within a particular country be attributed to that country? And if not, what are the consequences and responsibilities of a nation state when cyber attacks are determined to have originated from within its borders?

Over time, our nation has become highly dependent on networks and information systems to conduct essential operations. This technology has become simultaneously one of our most important sources of competitive advantage and one of our most serious strategic vulnerabilities. We have had twenty years to build a system of cyber defense to protect ourselves, and we have failed. Outside of the Department of Defense, no one has undertaken the responsibility of protecting our cyber assets, and today we lack an understanding of how to apportion that responsibility. Without a strategic defense doctrine, and with so many questions left unanswered, the threat of cyber war has become not only more likely, but also much more dangerous. The areas to defend are immense, the attack vectors are constantly changing, and our vulnerability is unacceptably high.

At a recent conference in Brussels, US Deputy Secretary of Defense William Lynn declared that we are currently engaged in an ongoing, accelerating "advanced persistent attack."[i] NATO allies must build a "cyber shield" to deter these attacks. In a recent article in Foreign Affairs, Lynn said US military and civilian networks are already targets of nation states' sponsored attacks. In response he calls for close cooperation with our allies and an expanded role for the National Security Agency (NSA) to monitor both domestic and international communications.[ii]

Army General Keith Alexander, who heads both US Cyber Command and the National Security Agency, agrees. There is "a real probability" that the United States "will be hit with a destructive attack," he said, "and we have to be ready for it." In a statement before congress, General Alexander warned, "The need is great, and there is no time to lose, as attacks and their potential effects would not discriminate between military and civilian users."[iii]

Such portent from our most senior leadership in the Department of Defense must be heard by Congress and the President. As in the Cold War, the risk of catastrophic outcome is unacceptably high, and there is too much at stake for this warning to be ignored. So, how should we respond? We must engage immediately to establish policy in five critical areas:

First, we must reestablish our strategic defense doctrine to counter the emerging threat. Furthermore, let's be certain to debate the real requirements, or we will risk ending up with an inappropriate structure. Difficult questions must be addressed such as: how do we monitor and protect the public internet while at the same time balance our essential democratic freedoms? When should a cyber attack be declared an act of war? When is a cyber attack not an act of war and the legitimate domain of law enforcement? What is the role of civilian businesses versus the government? How do we apportion the responsibilities to defend the various battle spaces?

Second, the scope of our cyber security initiatives must evolve to prioritize database protection. For years network-centric approaches have dominated our cyber security agenda, and today "super secure" networks form the vanguard of protection for our most critical infrastructure assets. Yet successful attacks and threat levels remain on the rise. Why? Because our adversaries are attacking where our defenses are the weakest! Verizon Business reports that databases were the source of 92 percent of records lost in 2009. We must close this critical gap and protect our data where it lives—in the database.

Third, we must examine and create the authorities for conflict in the information age. While it is clear that the Department of Homeland Security is responsible to defend our nondefense related government networks and databases, who is responsible for defending the critical infrastructure that operates in the private sector? And of equal importance, what are the authorities granted to the private sector to defend itself? When confronted by the apparent state-sponsored "aurora" attacks from China, Google responded much like a cyber militia executing its own strategic defense doctrine. But what authorities exist to govern the cyber militia? Should industry (Google) be granted the authority to actively defend itself against the first point of enemy presence? If an active defensive capability is not authorized for the private sector, then why not? Today, no other authority is in place to defend them.

Fourth, it is universally recognized that the Department of Defense (DOD) and the NSA maintain our most formidable capability for cyber security. That umbrella of protection must be extended to include our entire critical infrastructure, including that which resides within the US private sector. The private sector continues to make progress locking down critical infrastructure and sensitive data, but we must admit that the pace of progress is too slow, and today we still remain unacceptably vulnerable. Our nation cannot compromise when it comes to protecting our power grids, financial systems, and critical industrial complex from a devastating online attack. The technical challenges of extending the DOD protection umbrella are important, but not insurmountable. Political challenges, on the other hand, may prove more difficult. As we take action to achieve appropriate levels of defense, the American people must also be satisfied that their constitutional rights and freedoms will not be undermined in the process.

The fifth area of policy debate must address enhanced authorities for the oversight and regulation of information systems where the general welfare of the public is at stake. Many private enterprises and institutions properly lock down their sensitive data and IT infrastructure today simply because it is the right thing to do. Other businesses are proactive in defending themselves because they seek a competitive advantage. Unfortunately, the vast majority of businesses remain vulnerable because they are focused on other priorities, and this is unlikely to change until a proper system of incentives and enforceable mandates is put in place.

Congress currently has before it several bills to address the issue, and we must decide which, if any, should anchor our policy. Some have recommended draconian measures such as a Presidential authority for an internet "kill switch." Opponents argue that such measures amount to an assault on freedom of speech and freedom of the press. Regardless, the necessary standards and authorities must be put in place before meaningful progress can be achieved.

Time is of the essence, and the hope for cyber peace hangs in the balance. We must not delay any longer. It is imperative that we rapidly establish a new doctrine of strategic defense for cyber war. In the meantime, we should do all that we can to ensure trusted database security solutions are in place to protect our strategic coin—the knowledge contained in our databases.

Kenneth A. Minihan
Lieutenant General, United States Air Force (Retired)

INTRODUCTION

Databases contain our most valuable economic, personal, and government information. It is critical, therefore, that we protect such sensitive information in order to safeguard businesses, individuals, political systems, and human rights worldwide. When we save the database, we save the world. Why? Because when data stores are compromised, our society is at risk.

But if databases are so critical, why are they are so vulnerable? What happened along the way that allowed us to leave our most critical assets unprotected?

It is now cliché to say, "The Internet changed everything!" However, with the advent of the World Wide Web, humanity gained free and unlimited access to vast amounts of information and resources. Grandmothers became email-armed netizens. Amazon.com launched e-commerce. Google became the most valuable company on the planet. And the Internet challenged the Iranian Revolutionary Council during Iran's 2009 Presidential elections as social media tools such as Twitter and Facebook exposed the upheaval, turbulence, and civil unrest.

E-commerce has thrived, and the Web offers millions of people unlimited access to information, but this new era of business is also accompanied by new threats. At the turn of the century, high-profile scandals and business failures (such as Enron and MCI WorldCom) became watershed events calling for the broad adoption of enhanced corporate governance and risk management. In 1997, the US Congress approved the Sarbanes-Oxley Act (SOX) to ensure that public companies implement and maintain robust internal control processes, and to require that management and independent auditors attest to their effectiveness.

This same period also ushered in the harsh and unprecedented age of computer hacking. What began as entertainment in a movie called *War Games* starring Mathew Broderick soon evolved into a global campaign of cyber terrorism that has cost corporations and individuals billions of dollars. Today, the simple act of opening an email from an unknown source is a high-risk endeavor. The dictionary definitions of "worm" and "Trojan" have been rewritten, and many organizations now employ a key new executive—The Chief Information Security Officer (CISO)—whose job focus is to avoid SQL injections attacks, a new kind of pain that is arguably more agonizing than anything administered in a doctor's office. In 2008 and 2009, over 428 million database records were breached[iv], costing companies an average of $204 per exposed record.[v]

Will the next World War be fought as a cyber war? In a January 21, 2008 interview with The New Yorker Magazine, former US Director of National Intelligence Michael McConnell stated that the Department of Defense currently is detecting approximately three million unauthorized probes on its computer networks every day.[vi] In December 2009, the White House announced the appointment of Howard A. Schmidt—a former Chief Security Officer at Microsoft and at eBay—to the role of Cyber Security Coordinator. For the first time, this powerful role has direct access to the President of the United States. No longer just a Hollywood creation, cyber terrorism has become very real and very dangerous to governments, businesses, and civil society.

What are these hackers after? The answer is that they seek sensitive data—specifically corporate, government, and Personally Identifiable Information (PII). Whether they seek illegal profit, financial gain, military or competitive advantage, these criminals want access to our data. And how can we stop them from wreaking such havoc on our society? While we may never be truly safe from the threat of hackers, we can take effective actions and fight back by protecting data at its source—in the database. We must rise up to this challenge. *Save The Database, Save The World!*

But there are over ten million databases now in production across the globe and less than ten percent maintain effective database SRC controls.[vii] How can we *Save The Database, Save The World!* when the criminal hacking community enjoys such a target-rich environment with so many soft points to attack? With limited available investment, resource constraints, and a myriad of conflicting priorities, the challenge to defend ourselves is substantial, but not insurmountable.

Successful data protection strategies and solutions must:

- *Span the enterprise*; be highly scalable and capable of protecting large numbers of heterogeneous database servers deployed across global networks.

- *Deliver reliability, serviceability, and manageability* because the mission-critical nature of this complex task demands it.

- *Offer affordability* to ensure low total cost of ownership (TCO), high return on investment (ROI), and fast time-to-value.

These are the foundations of *Save The Database, Save The World! Database Security, Risk, and Compliance in the Age of Cyber War.*

"Where's the information?"

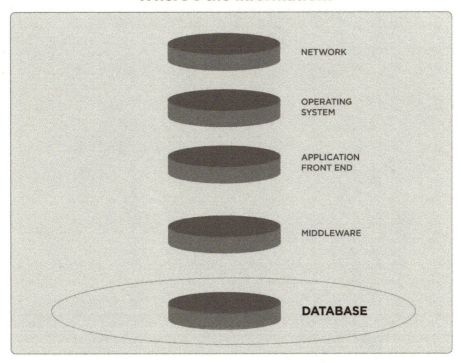

Figure 1: Sensitive information travels across all layers of the enterprise-computing stack, but lives in the database.

Chapter 1

THE GATHERING STORM

"Four hundred and twenty-eight million records were breached between 2008 and 2009."[viii]

E-Business or Out of Business

The Internet drives enormous economic and social growth worldwide, but this growth also yields enormous data protection challenges. Mobile apps, handheld browsers, ubiquitous Wi-Fi connections, Internet-facing Web apps, and a flood of virtual private network (VPN) connections all challenge the adequacy of perimeter and "super secure" network strategies. This new set of security challenges has given rise not only to new technologies, but also to new sets of organizational tasks and responsibilities. Perhaps no new role carries more responsibility than the Chief Information Security Officer (CISO), who is tasked to work across functional business units and establish SRC policies to protect enterprise information.

Security, risk and compliance (SRC) strategies were far simpler in the pre-Internet era, and few companies had even dreamt of creating a CISO position. Most information security strategies simply followed a "no trespassing" approach designed to keep unauthorized persons out of a company's technology infrastructure. Perhaps no system epitomized this strategy better than IBM's Systems Network Architecture (SNA), which was designed to support user access in the mainframe-computing era of the 1980's. SNA was so successful at securing enterprise infrastructure (primarily by keeping unauthorized users out) that the cybercrime and hacker lexicons that are so prevalent on the front pages today did not even exist.

But then the dot-com era and the Internet arrived and turned enterprise computing architecture on its head. IT executives were challenged to rearchitect computing infrastructures (literally overnight) from models designed to keep people "out" to e-commerce models designed to bring as many people as possible "in." The new goal was to provision access for anyone with a Web browser to applications running on the corporate computing infrastructure. Every business process—from sales to procurement—required Web-enabled reengineering. "E-business or out of business" became the catch phrase of the new century, and strategies to secure enterprise infrastructure were changed forevermore.

Then along came Enron. How could the growth of one of the most successful Fortune 500 companies in history be built almost entirely upon fraud and deception? How was it possible for traditional corporate auditors to be fooled so completely, and for traditional oversight controls to be circumvented so successfully? Enron had ascended the Fortune 500 faster than any company in history, and in only a few short years became a multi-billion-dollar juggernaut. But then, upon the ultimate disclosure of wrongdoing at Enron, billions of dollars of wealth dissipated into thin air, and, at Internet speed, the dot-com era came to a crashing halt. All of a sudden the e-business model, which fueled one of the most dramatic economic expansions in world history, turned into a bubble and burst. Soon the US Congress enacted Sarbanes-Oxley (SOX), ushering in a new set of demands by government for transparency and oversight against bad business behavior and poor internal controls. Following SOX, an alphabet soup of new compliance regulations appeared, including NERC, FERC, FISMA, DISA STIG, GLBA, PCI DSS, HIPAA, and the HITECH Act. The parade of new regulations has since expanded to the state government level and worldwide. More than just guidelines to achieve audit compliance, many of these mandates carry enforcement provisions that cannot be ignored.

Audit Requirements	SOX	PCI	HIPAA	FISMA (NIST 800-53)	GLBA	BASEL II	DIACAP (DISA-STIG)	NERC
Complete Inventory of In-Scope Databases	✓	✓	✓	✓	✓	✓	✓	✓
Vulnerability and Configuration Assessment	✓	✓	✓	✓	✓	✓	✓	✓
User Rights Review and Separation of Duties	✓	✓	✓	✓	✓	✓	✓	✓
Threat Monitoring		✓	✓	✓	✓		✓	✓
Privileged Activity Monitoring	✓	✓	✓	✓	✓	✓	✓	✓

Figure 2: The major compliance regulations driving database audit requirements and protection policies.

From Perimeter Security to Defense in Depth

The "no trespassing" zones of the 1980's transformed into cyber malls where Internet shoppers were encouraged to come and go as they pleased to browse and conduct e-commerce. With the seismic shift from mainframe computing to "open systems" over the past thirty years, SNA gave way to TCP/IP networks, and information security teams began to rearchitect their strategies. First to arrive were perimeter defense firewall technologies, based on the hard-won lessons of attacks arriving at enterprise's front door. But as the Internet now meant that the goal had shifted from keeping outsiders "out" to enticing as much traffic as possible "in," CISOs moved to a more flexible and accommodating strategy called defense in depth. In a fresh new approach, security strategy was developed and deployed in layers. Viewed logically from the outside in, network perimeters, operating systems, and databases became autonomous layers requiring separate and distinct policies of protection. Layered defense in depth strategies have since become the foundation to securing corporate computing infrastructures as World Wide Web browsers navigate and conduct e-business. But, as any computer security professional knows, no defense is ever bulletproof. Hackers are always one step ahead, devising new vectors for attack.

Layered Enterprise Data Security Model

Database protection is the last line of defense in a comprehensive enterprise security framework

Figure 3: Layered defense in depth enterprise data security model

Protecting Data Where It Lives—In the Database

Today, less than 10% of the world's databases are locked down with database SRC controls[ix]. Common sense dictates that attackers will strike where the defenses are the weakest, and it did not take long for the attackers to shift their focus from networks to the applications and databases themselves. From rudimentary password guessing to sophisticated SQL injection attacks, hackers began to exploit their targets by identifying authorized points of access to penetrate the application layer and the ultimate target: the database. After all, the database is where sensitive data lives.

It is significant that many attacks aren't affected by perimeters. In fact, security experts maintain that the threat from within is growing fast, and internal threats are more common now than ever before. Some suggest the high rate of unemployment and the large number of disaffected workers stemming from the 2009 economic downturn has contributed. Verizon Business's Global Investigative Response Team found individuals with insider knowledge of organizations accounted for 48 percent of all breaches in 2009, and that number has been increasing." [x] The threat from within, however, is by no means isolated to disaffected workers. All authorized users—including employees, customers, suppliers, and other business partners who have been granted application access—must be included in the threat analysis. Motive and willingness to act are all that is needed for insiders to become malicious cyber terrorists. Of course, not all inappropriate insider activity is malicious. A significant number of breaches can be attributed to honest mistakes by well-meaning employees who have both appropriate and inappropriate access. But make no mistake: the unethical hackers are out there (or more aptly, they're already inside).

The information security landscape is forever evolving, and the threat to sensitive data continues to increase as attacks are moving to the database where records can be harvested en masse. The target has shifted to the place where the data resides—in the database itself. With distributed databases in place to provide ubiquitous access to data, this threat can no longer be managed solely by securing networks and perimeters. All information needs to be locked down, particularly in regard to database access.

Defense in depth means multi-layered countermeasures are now a requirement, especially at the database layer. Authorized access is expanding to a wider range of users—including employees, contractors, suppliers, partners, and third-party vendors to name a few. Business partners driven to optimize results are reengineering their networks and applications to interoperate, requiring that close attention be paid to security vulnerability. The extended enterprise means that the once-reliable and clear definition of an "authorized user" has begun to blur, and the ability of "super secure" networks and perimeter security strategies to protect the enterprise has been called into question.

So-called "super secure" networks and perimeter defenses offer little or no protection when intruders operate from *inside* the firewall, and many enterprises often have little to no protection in place at the database and application layer. Perimeter security is ineffective against the threat from within and therefore insufficient to protect organizations against a breach. Poor access controls, excessive permission grants, patch gaps, and configuration vulnerabilities— which provide attack vectors for hackers, crackers, and malicious or careless insiders—are the new "ground zero" for security teams and a new point of attack where defenses are the weakest.

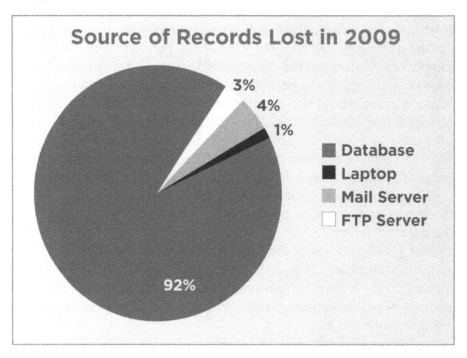

Figure 4: The database was the source of 92% of records lost in 2009[xi]

Application and database security can be confusing, and complexity is the watchword of database SRC. What is database security, anyway? How is it deployed? How long will it take to deploy? And what resources will it require? Moreover, how will it affect application availability, and will application access and latency become an issue? What are the regulatory requirements driven by SOX and NIST 800-53? What about other compliance requirements that affect our organization such as PCI,

HIPAA, and the DISA STIG? What are the database auditing requirements for SAS 70? And which security frameworks are applicable to our organization such as ISO 27002 (formerly 17799), ISO 27001, CIS, and COBIT? Organizations with international operations face a complex set of challenges, having to identify, track, and demonstrate compliance and controls against a matrix of overlapping (and often confusing) regulatory and audit requirements.

The impact of this complex, new and evolving security threat means different things to different stakeholders:

Database Administrators (DBAs): In addition to being responsible for the maintenance and performance of all mission-critical databases, DBAs are now being told they must take on additional tasks including laborious scrubbing of data logs in search of anomalous activity; user entitlement review; scripting to manage configuration vulnerabilities and patch gaps; as well as information assurance to certify that databases conform to established SRC policy. Configuration changes to remediate vulnerabilities must be tested to ensure application availability.

Internal Auditors: Databases are now included in the audit scope. Primary responsibilities include analysis and attestation of database entitlements; access control based on least privilege; privileged user activity auditing; separation of duty analysis; compliance with regulatory requirements; patch and configuration management practices according to established process and/or policy. These are all now compulsory audit requirements at the database layer.

Security Operations: CISO teams must now assure that a full life cycle approach to database SRC is in place, including the discovery and inventory of database assets; performance of initial entitlement reviews; separation of duty and least privilege analysis; establishment of database SRC policies; identification, assessment, and mitigation of security vulnerabilities; safeguarding of the enterprise against breaches by both authorized and unauthorized users.

IT Executives: Top management is responsible for prioritizing SRC initiatives; assessing the overall vulnerability posture against compulsory compliance regulations (especially for public companies); ensuring the protection of critical corporate database assets; protecting brand and shareholder interests through information assurance (IA) initiatives.

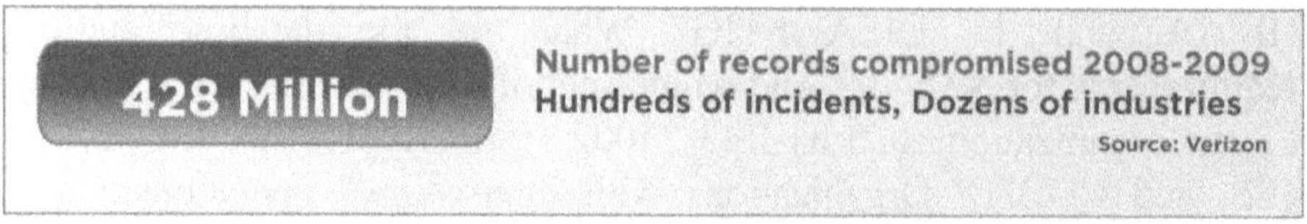

Figure 5:Number of records compromised in 2008 and 2009.[xii]

Across every organization, the impact of this evolving threat environment is being felt. Whether driven by external threats, insider threats, or auditor findings, the challenges of database SRC have changed key roles and responsibilities. No longer can we rely on "super secure" networks to safeguard our sensitive data. We must add measures to protect the data where it lives—in the database.

Chapter 2

THE ENEMY

"I never gave a thought to the millions of people whose lives I impacted." – Albert Gonzalez[xiii]

Criminals

Originally identified as mischief-makers and thrill-seeking computer geeks, hackers have evolved into highly skilled and organized criminals. Lured by the opportunity of financial gain and notoriety in the black hat community, criminal networks armed with the most sophisticated cyber tool sets have emerged worldwide. While it is unclear exactly how much theft and damage has occurred, the stories surrounding the known exploits of databases have made dramatic headlines.

Perhaps no cyber perpetrator has achieved greater infamy than Albert Gonzalez. Gonzalez was reported to be computer savvy by age eight, a successful hacker of government computer systems in India and NASA by high school, and a rising star on Shadowcrew.com (a cyber crime messaging board) by age twenty-two. At the time of his first bust, Gonzalez and his accomplices were accused of operating an international crime ring focused on ATM and credit card fraud. To avoid jail time, Gonzalez began working for the Secret Service as an informant and, ironically, helped the US Department of Justice and the Secret Service build a case against those involved with Shadowcrew.[xiv]

Unbeknownst to the government, while on their payroll, Gonzalez was also working with his crew of hackers on new and even more lucrative hacking schemes. Upon learning of his betrayal, many government officials who worked closely with Gonzalez during his time with the Secret Service felt that he was "essentially a double agent."[xv]

Originally indicted by a federal grand jury for breaking into T. J. Maxx's credit card processing operations, Albert Gonzalez and his team also allegedly executed breaches at many of the most well-known companies in the United States; including Dave & Buster's, BJ's Wholesale Club, OfficeMax, Hannaford Brothers, 7-Eleven, and J. C. Penney. Gonzalez, while being one of the government's most valuable cybercrime informants, was also responsible for the largest data breach in history. He hacked over one hundred million credit cards from Heartland Payment Systems. Once in possession of the stolen credit card information, Gonzalez and his gang reportedly sold the valuable data on the Internet black market. [xvi]

By the time his run was over, Albert Gonzalez was convicted of some of the most explosive crimes in computer hacking history. He was named in three Federal indictments and accused of stealing and reselling over 150 million credit card and ATM numbers between 2005 and 2007. On March 25, 2010 Gonzalez was sentenced to twenty years in Federal prison. [xvii]

Figure 6: Albert Gonzalez[xviii]

But as notorious as Albert Gonzalez became as details of the corporate plights of the Heartland Payment Systems and TJX breaches made headlines, the bigger question may be, "What about the ones who never got caught or were not detected?" Researchers have only speculated, because there is no opportunity to prove otherwise, that the biggest source of fraud may lie with the undiscovered and unreported cases. From the execution of fraudulent transactions to cases of insider knowledge and outright heists of sensitive data for personal gain, those who have breached our databases illegally have waged war across our commerce system, and the damage they have caused should be characterized as nothing less than disastrous.

Privileged Users and Insiders

One of the more onerous and challenging aspects of the new threat environment is protecting our database assets from privileged users and insiders. In order to achieve compliance, organizations are finding themselves under increased pressure to safeguard and track users with privileged access to sensitive data. Privileged users can be anyone whose permissions to access and manipulate the database exceed those required to perform their job. Privileged users are generally thought of as DBAs, super users, or system administrators with universal access. But in fact, privileged users are anyone whose access rights to the database are excessive. Since privileged users are typically the personnel tasked with watching for suspicious, malicious, or unauthorized activity, while at the same time enjoying levels of access beyond which oversight is possible, they are sometimes referred to as "the fox watching the hen house." As a classic separation of duty control violation, IT auditors seek processes and procedures for monitoring privileged user activity as a compensating control to their otherwise uncontrolled access to sensitive data.

According to Verizon, "the percentage of cases that involved insiders rose to 48 percent, an increase of 26 percent over the previous year." [xix] How do we classify an insider? Insiders are defined in three categories:

- *Authorized and intelligent*—those that use IT resources appropriately
- *Authorized and "stupid"*—those that make mistakes that may appear as malicious or fraudulent

- *Unauthorized and malicious*—users that mask either their identity or their behavior or both

The first two categories can be identified and tracked with rights management and identity management systems. The latter cannot.

Cyber researcher Bryan Krekel reports, "The amount of breaches that exploit authentication in some manner is a problem…Perhaps this is because they know we don't monitor user activity very well. Perhaps it's just the easiest way in the door. Whatever the reason, we have some work to do here."[xx]

Organizations may categorize their user accounts differently, but we can generally view privileged accounts as falling into one of these four categories:

- *Authorized privileged user accounts* may include database administrators, system administrators, database owners, consultants, contractors, and outsourced developers. These accounts need to be identified, and normal activity needs to be tracked. Moreover, these accounts should be monitored for suspicious or unauthorized activity.

- *Authorized user accounts with excessive privileges* may include users who have transferred to other positions in the organization but still retain the privileged rights granted from the previous job. Authorized users also include individuals who have been granted excessive privileges by role inheritance, by accident, or by default. IT security personnel should clearly identify these accounts and adjust rights as necessary.

- *Unauthorized user accounts with excessive privileges* include users that have escalated their own privileges surreptitiously. These user accounts also represent a serious threat, and database access should be revoked or configured correctly. A routine entitlement review should be performed, and user activity should be monitored in real time for evidence of anomalous behavior.

- *Legacy application accounts* are homegrown/custom applications that have privileged accounts hard-coded into the application. These accounts cannot be revoked, nor can their privileged status be changed. Such accounts must be identified, their normal activity should be tracked, and, most importantly, they should be monitored for suspicious or unauthorized activity.

In some cases, privileged users and insiders can be effectively managed through strengthened controls and improved oversight. In other cases, the threat from privileged users and insiders is more dangerous. So long as organizations continue to operate on the fundamental assumption that authorized users do not pose risk, database security will continue to be a major source of fraud, theft, and compliance failure.

Warriors

More recently, the fear of state-sponsored cybercrime has arisen. If the US Department of Defense is reporting three million unauthorized probes on its networks every day[xxi], then who is responsible? Is a cyber attack perpetrated by one country against another just a crime, or is it an act of war? Are we *currently* engaged in a cyber war? And is this war raging undeclared? What happens if a cyber attack against private business is found to be state sponsored, such as the "Aurora" allegations that Chinese government operatives hacked into Google and other global business entities? Which government body carries the responsibility to respond to such attacks? The Department of Defense? The Department of Homeland Security? The United Nations? NATO?

So far, cyber war has never been publicly declared, although the evidence of state-sponsored attacks is overwhelming. Partly on account of the cyber hysteria promoted by press reports and partly based on hard evidence, specific accusations of state-sponsored cyber attacks abound. Israel, Russia, Iran, China, the United States, and a number of Eastern European countries are most frequently cited as cyber war combatants. For example the denial of service and botnet attacks during the Russia-Georgia conflict in the summer of 2008 and the Russia-Estonia conflict in 2007 are both widely attributed as state-sponsored cyber war engagements. In the lead up to both US invasions of Iraq, not only were Iraqi air defenses and command and control capabilities substantially degraded through US cyber attacks, it was nearly impossible to make a phone call on a public network.

Perhaps no country has been cited more frequently in recent news reports than China with regard to cyber war involvement. People's Liberation Army (PLA) Major General Huang Yongyin has called the Internet "a battlefield without gunpowder,"[xxii] and considerable attention is now focused on the PLA's 3rd Department, a well-formed cyber division that Western military analysts estimate to staff over 130,000 cyber warriors.[xxiii] In October 2009, the US-China Economic and Security Review Commission released the "Report on the Capability of the People's Republic of China to Conduct Cyber Warfare and Computer Network Exploitation," which points out the following:

> The People's Republic of China (PRC) is a decade into a sweeping military modernization program that has fundamentally transformed its ability to fight high tech wars…This doctrinal focus is providing the impetus for the development of an advanced Information Warfare (IW) capability, the stated goal of which is to establish control of an adversary's information flow and maintain dominance in the battle space.[xxiv]

Figure 7: Hacker school enrollment advertisements seen in the streets of Wuhan.[xxv]

The paper presents "a comprehensive open source assessment of China's capability to conduct computer network operations (CNO) both during peacetime and periods of conflict." The data collected in the report and the conclusions suggest that capability of the PLA to wage cyber war is substantial.[xxvi]

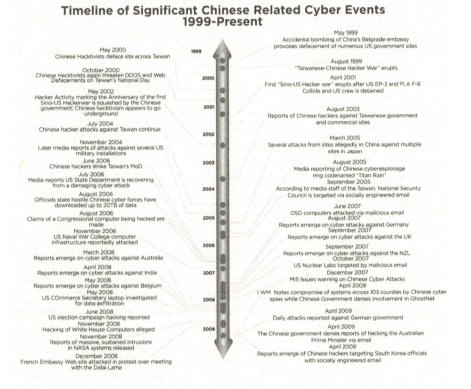

Figure 8:Timeline of Significant China Related Cyber Events[xxvii]

As unwilling combatants in an undeclared war, public and private enterprises are left in a precarious position. In the Aurora attacks in early 2010 the Chinese military was alleged to have attacked Google's internal IT systems (in addition to several other large US corporations). Rather than launch a cyber counter attack, Google management decided to make a public stand for Internet freedom. After considerable negotiation, Google decided to exit the Chinese market on account of China's insistence on censoring Google's search engine. Other companies and organizations may not find the cyber war exit door so gracefully.

Alan Paller, Research Director at the SANS Institute, reported in early 2010 that thirty CEOs of major US utility companies attended closed briefings by senior FBI officials, who told them that their information systems environments had been declared "contested territories." The CEOs were told that the attackers "used the same techniques as those used by nation states in attacks on the defense industrial base and federal government systems." The CEOs were further advised that any delays implementing defenses against the attacks would be viewed by their shareholders as "negligence."[xxviii]

Paller summarized his report with the following stark conclusion: "Cyber security is an arms race where each new advance by attackers is met by better defenses. For several years, utilities have acted as if compliance to the US Department of Defense's Critical Infrastructure Protection (CIP) program was synonymous with security. That put them deeply at risk. Now that they know they must do much more, including active policy enforcement, encryption, two factor access control, and deep forensic monitoring, many are moving ahead forcefully to shore up their defenses." [xxix]

But not everyone responsible for the protection of US cyber interests agrees with the extent of the threat. In fact, some leaders maintain that the threat is overstated or even overhyped. In an interview, Obama Administration Cyber Security Coordinator Howard Schmidt said that he "isn't buying into the grim forecasts that the United States is ill-prepared to defend the government's and nation's critical information assets from an immense virtual attack by political adversaries or cyber criminals." Mr. Schmidt's comments were in direct response to remarks made by former National Intelligence Director Michael McConnell that the United States would lose a cyber war if it were fought today.[xxx] One thing, however, is for certain: until we achieve a consensus that we *do* in fact face a clear and present danger, any progress made to strengthen our defenses will be slow, and the global risk to society will continue to increase. [xxxi]

Attribution

How do we defend against an attacker whose identity may be unknown? Unlike in conventional war, where enemy attackers are easily identified by the insignia on their uniform, cyber attackers may operate not only unseen, but their point of presence may be impossible to ascertain or prove. Some suggest that cyber warriors should be treated as "illegal combatants." Attribution without proof becomes nothing more than an allegation of involvement, and in cyber space, one rarely finds a smoking gun. Effective law enforcement must be based on more than just suspicions, and the complexity of cyber space means that fingerprints and traditional forensics are often not available.

Database breach forensic investigations seek to identity the "true user" who perpetrated an attack, but the fog of cyber war often obscures such efforts. Application user sessions accessing databases are sometimes managed by connection pools, which obfuscate "true user" identities. As these users traverse the tiers of application and database servers, the access credentials of "John Doe" may be transformed to "APPUSER1." Database firewall technologies seek to track these users by offering hints of "true user" identity, but forensic proof requires attribution beyond the shadow of a doubt. No reasonable chance of false identification may exist.

Connection pooled event correlation thus has become more of a black art than a science. Busy applications that perform small, frequent database transactions rapidly connect and drop sessions, freeing pooled resources for the next application user. As a result, time-stamped event correlation, even when tagged and logged by the application itself, may sometimes fail to definitively track "true users", especially in multi-application, heterogeneous environments. Consequently, database firewall technologies are generally ruled out as an evidentiary foundation for establishing "true user" identity.

Moreover, just because a database log is able to display the access history of a credentialed user does not necessarily mean that the owner of those credentials is the attacker. Authorized credentials can be stolen, misused, or repurposed in any number of nefarious ways, further complicating attribution and the identity of "true users."

Our Own Worst Enemy

Despite the dangers of opposing cyber divisions and cyber mafias, we may in fact be our own worst enemy in many cases. Immense organizational impetus is required to mobilize defenses and form the columns of corporate militia required to effectively defend against cyber attacks. Information security represents a complex problem involving the integration of many technologies across many layers of the computing stack. Networks, server operating systems, endpoints, applications, and databases all require unique focus to ensure protection. As soon as countermeasures are established and deployed against known threats, new sets of viruses, worms, trojans, and vulnerabilities are discovered. An effective cyber security strategy starts with the basic premise that the attackers are *always* one step ahead, and no protection system is ever bulletproof. Effective systems of protection require management commitment, careful planning, adequate funding, and focused security teams.

Threat awareness and resolve varies amongst those tasked with the responsibility for cyber security. Some organizations, perhaps those already stung by a breach or critical audit finding, regard cyber security as an imperative, and deploy appropriate resources without compromise. However, in other organizations, IT security strategy is a hedge game grounded in actuarial risk management. Competing priorities may create conflicts within defense strategies, limiting the effectiveness of the overall program. Executives faced with budget constraints may decide to defer critical investments, and corporate governance teams faced with multiple imperatives may simply make poor decisions regarding priorities. But avoidance must be declared unacceptable, and organizations must face up to the task. Weak passwords, misconfigurations, patch gaps, and unattested user entitlements must be fixed, or we risk being overrun by unseen attackers.

While the extent of our preparedness is often in debate, one thing is for certain: the enemy is now more sophisticated and capable of inflicting significant harm than ever before. Will Google prevail in its strategy to stand behind Internet freedom? Certainly the cost of exiting one of the world's largest markets is great. But in the absence of a federal declaration of cyber war, organizations must mobilize and defend themselves. For some organizations enforcement provisions from industry-backed groups such as PCI and government mandates like SOX will stimulate appropriate action. For others the bar is set higher. Proactive organizations are preparing for cyber war now. Others have mistakenly chosen to believe that such threats are isolated, and would never happen to them. No matter to whom the claxon calls, the cyber war has not only started—it is raging. And the database is "ground zero."

Chapter 3

A FALSE SENSE OF SECURITY

"84 percent of organizations believe their security is adequate, yet 56 percent of the same organizations have experienced a breach in the last year."[xxxii]

Databases Are Under Attack!

It may take a skilled hacker only minutes to crack into a database and exit undetected with hordes of valuable, sensitive data. What's more, these intruders are not amateurs out for a weekend conquest or a reason to brag on clandestine message boards. Many are hard-nosed, professional criminals. Others are highly skilled, well trained, and organized cyber warriors seeking to inflict massive harm. So what are organizations doing about it? The simple answer is this: not enough!

An Enterprise Strategy Group study recently surveyed over two hundred corporate and government organizations, and the results were not as expected:

- Forty-three percent of corporate databases store confidential data.
- Eighty-four percent feel that their database security is adequate.
- Fifty-six percent of those organizations have experienced a breach in the last 12 months.
- Seventy-three percent predict that database attacks will increase.

How in the world can 84 percent of these organizations believe their security is adequate, yet 56 percent of the same organizations have experienced a breach in the last year? Whether these companies have a false sense of security or simply a case of denial, 73 percent of those same companies predict that attacks on their databases are accelerating.[xxxiii]

We hear nonstop reports of database breaches, but let's not forget that these are only the ones that have been discovered and reported. The public admission of a significant operational failure (such as a customer data loss) invites not only bad press, but risks a breakdown of customer trust as well. Organizations seeking to limit public knowledge of security breaches often suppress such information, unless the law compels them to disclose it.

Other organizations, lacking adequate protection, may not even realize that a breach has occurred. "One of the biggest problems is that many database attacks are not known about," says Noel Yuhanna, principal analyst with The Forrester Group. "The typical database may have 15,000 to 20,000 connections per second. It's not humanly possible to know what all of these [connections] are doing." [xxxiv]

The task of manually reviewing and analyzing terabytes of audit log data on a regular basis is indeed impossible, and therefore no one does the job. As a result, there are no statistics available on how many breaches go unreported. For every breach that is discovered (and reported), it is likely that a higher number go undiscovered or unreported.

Naysayers who suggest that databases don't need to be locked down perpetuate this false sense of security. "Our networks are 'super secure,'" they say. "Why bother to lock them down if unauthorized users cannot connect in the first place?" While the fortress mentality may even sound reasonable, closer examination reveals that such a perspective is not only naïve, but also reckless.

Despite the myriad of defenses deployed at the perimeter—including authentication, network intrusion detection (IDS), endpoint hardening, and white-listing—it only takes a single virtual private network (VPN) connection in the wrong hands, and that person can perpetrate a catastrophic attack. Every day hundreds of millions of Internet users access secure networks through a VPN. Once they have access to the network, many well-known attack vectors become qualified on-ramps to the database. Weak passwords, entitlement grants to "PUBLIC", patch gaps, and misconfigurations present a rich opportunity for cyber criminals to launch SQL injections, buffer overflows, and privilege escalations.

Just like the successful pickpocket, who can take a wallet without the victim even noticing they've become a target, cyber criminals use phishing attacks, social engineering, and other fraudulent means for acquiring passwords and usernames to gain credentialed network access. Once they have network access, hackers are then free to target databases, searching for and taking any valuable, sensitive data they discover.

As a first line of defense, network perimeters serve an important role in deterring attacks, but no organization should consider such a thin line of defense adequate.

Just as the Maginot Line failed to stop the German invasion of France in World War II, "super secure" networks are not capable of securing sensitive corporate data. To prevent a frontal assault, France constructed a line of concrete fortifications, tank traps, artillery emplacements, and machine gun bunkers along its borders with Germany and Italy. Thought to be impregnable, the Maginot Line failed as a military strategy because the German army maneuvered around the fortifications in a flanking attack launched through Belgium.[xxxv] They invaded France in just days.

Today, "super secure" networks bear much too much resemblance to the Maginot Line. The strength of "super secure" networks is that only authorized users with proper credentials are able to gain access. But the problem lies in the fact that many attacks do not require fraudulent network access in the first place. John Pescatore of the Gartner Group estimates that most security incidents that cause loss to enterprises, rather than mere annoyance, typically involve insiders. Enterprises, therefore, must broaden their approach beyond only securing Internet-exposed applications and servers.[xxxvi] Users with authorized credentials can flank "super secure" networks just as the German army did when attacking the Maginot Line.

The statistic that 84 percent of companies believe their defenses are adequate is disturbing because security best practice says that even activity inside the firewalled perimeter must be considered a potential point of attack. If companies provide all employees with network access, they must assume that some will use their credentials maliciously. They must also assume that cyber criminals will obtain authorized credentials fraudulently, and that other risks, such as password attacks, are likely to succeed.

A False Sense of Cost

The size and scope of the threat is enormous, but the costs involved are even more staggering. Verizon reports that from 2008 to

2009, hundreds of incidents occurred, and over 428 million records were compromised. Out of that total, databases were the source of the breach 92 percent of the time.[xxxvii] Ponemon Institute research reports that the cost per exposed record has skyrocketed from $138 in 2005 to $204 per record lost in 2009.[xxxviii] In addition, corporations are forced to increase DBA resources and increase CISO and audit team staff to manage the ever-increasing threat. The research shows that cost of data loss has risen into the billions of dollars.

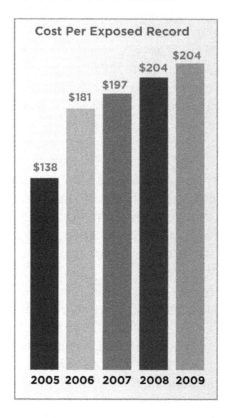

Figure 9: Cost per exposed record.[xxxix]

So far, no one has tackled the cost of partial protection or the cost incurred when companies expend funds to protect some computing assets, but others turn out to be the source of a breach. Brand damage and opportunity costs also add up as the attention gained from a data breach amounts to bad press. Other intangibles—such as public relations, corporate trust, customer attrition, and shareholder impacts—while hard to measure, may ultimately represent an even greater cost to an organization.

And let's not forget the consumer. The Cyber Security Industry Alliance reports, "The average victim of identity theft spends $834 and 77 hours to clear his or her name." [xl] No one is immune. Reports of database breaches come from a diverse set of companies across a range of industries.

Company/Organization	# of Affected Customers
Heartland Payment Systems	100,000,000
TJ Maxx	94,000,000
UCLA	800,000
Arkansas Dept. of Information Systems	807,000
DSW Shoe Warehouse	1,400,000
Bank of America	1,200,000
phpBB.com	400,000
Digital River	198,000
Card Systems	40,000,000
Lexis Nexis	310,000
Ameritrade	200,000
ChoicePoint	163,000
Peninsula Orthopedic Assoc.	100,000

Figure 10: Breaches by company and the number of affected customers.

A False Sense of Compliance

In September 2009 the Ponemon Institute released another report to determine "if Payment Card Industry Data Security Standard (PCI DSS) compliance improves organizational security." More specifically, Ponemon probed "how the move to comply with PCI affects an organization's strategy, tactics, and approach to achieve enterprise data protection and security." Once again, the findings defied expectations. From their survey of 517 US and international IT practitioners, Ponemon reported, "Seventy-one percent of companies do not treat PCI as a strategic initiative, and 79 percent have experienced a data breach." [xli]

Despite the fact that the PCI DSS standard was established to strengthen credit card security, and that it defines clear guidelines for merchants to improve credit card protection, the number of data breaches since it was established in June 2005 has continued to rise. The Ponemon survey raises the question of whether PCI and credit card merchants are doing enough to protect consumers, and confirms a false sense of compliance. Even though over three quarters of credit card merchants have been breached, Ponemon points out that "fifty-six percent of respondents do not believe compliance with PCI DSS improves their organization's data security posture." [xlii]

While PCI was launched with the greatest expectations, credit card security today still has not improved. In fact the problem has grown steadily worse. With so many of the largest breaches occurring at companies who claim compliance with PCI, clearly more needs to be done to strengthen standards. As a broad-based initiative, PCI DSS has yielded improvements, but conflicting interests and priorities regarding the enforcement of credit card security have compromised progress.

Should the enforcement of data security be mandated beyond industry regulatory initiatives such as PCI? The answer depends on how heavy a burden we should expect an industry to place upon itself. With billions of credit card dollars flowing through the system daily, card issuers and their merchants face an enormous responsibility to protect consumers. More importantly, the secure flow of commerce worldwide depends on data protection.

The ultimate accountability for data protection lies with the organizations who manage sensitive data. Whether additional oversight is warranted or not, breaches, audit findings, and compliance failures hurt business results, sometimes beyond repair. Consumers and shareholders increasingly will demand improved controls to protect their sensitive data.

The Weakest Link

It stands to reason that any security system only provides as much protection as its weakest link. Whether attacking a fort during ancient times, or planning an offensive in the cyber war, an attacker always searches for the weakest link. By probing defenses and analyzing response behaviors, the enemy seeks out soft points in order to identify where he or she can penetrate defenses most easily. While the "weakest link attack" is a key consideration of almost any IT defense strategy, it is often overlooked when it comes to database security, risk, and compliance.

When applied to database technology, the weakest link lexicon takes on a new meaning. Database links connect databases together into networks, enabling distributed queries and distributed processing of data. Compliance programs that fail to cover database links risk real world exposure since authorized users on one database may gain access to sensitive data on another database through database links. Database SRC programs that fail to include security for database links are limited by scope to partial protection.

Consider this scenario: a database SRC team is responsible to manage a network at a large bank which contains five database systems. Three of those databases are production systems that store and process sensitive financial information. The other two databases are development servers that are used to create and test enhancements for the production systems. The development systems never store live data, and all data imported from production is properly masked. The three production systems are thoroughly locked down and are annually certified for compliance. Since the two development systems are deemed out of scope and ignored, a critical security and access control issue has been missed by the database SRC team leaving the organization at risk and out-of-compliance.

Where is the vulnerability, and how did they miss it? Database links connecting the development and production databases facilitate the import of customer data. Under normal circumstances, the imported data is immediately masked. However, anyone with the right permissions on the development server can abuse these links to gain direct access to live production data. Since it was deemed out of scope, the development system was never secured. In fact, many development database instances are purposely configured for maximum convenience and left that way. In this case "GUEST" access was configured as "OPEN", and "PUBLIC" (every user) had powerful privileges including access to database links. Intruders are therefore able to log on to either of the development systems and collect all the customer data they desire through database links to the production servers. When an auditor finds this kind of vulnerability, there is an audit finding, and the company has to remove the threat immediately. When an attacker finds this kind of vulnerability, the results are significantly worse.

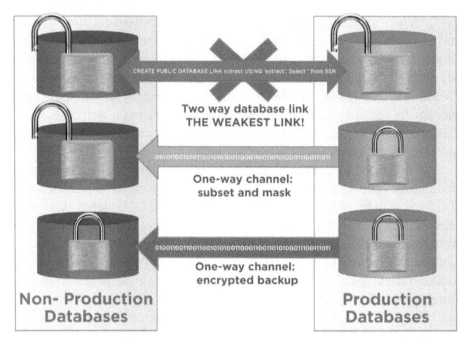

*Figure 11: A weakest link example; interaction between
production and nonproduction database instances.*

The rise of regulatory pressures in today's business environment has motivated many IT organizations to prioritize compliance above security. The shift is justified by the explanation that "If I'm compliant, I must therefore be secure." This view, however widely held, only contributes to the false sense of security.

Compliance policies generally designate sets of "target" database systems as "in-scope", because they house the sensitive data relevant to a specific regulation. For example, compliance policies supporting the Health Insurance Portability and Accountability Act (HIPAA) may only consider databases in scope that contain personally identifiable healthcare information. Therefore, other database systems not containing sensitive data specific to the HIPAA compliance regulation are often left out of scope. These systems not designated for HIPAA, but sharing a common network with other HIPAA target servers, can represent alluring vectors for attack. We must consider the least-secured databases on the network just as critical to the protection scope as "target" databases. Databases set up to manage the lunch menu or corporate softball roster may, in fact, be even higher-priority targets for hackers. Once penetrated, these databases can offer back door access to prized PCI or SOX servers through database links. Because they have fewer security controls deployed, these databases become the weakest link.

It is for this reason that some compliance standards, such as PCI DSS, mandate protection for all database systems residing on a network containing regulated data, rather than just those database systems known to house and process credit card data. This is an important requirement, but also difficult to measure and enforce. As a result, it is often overlooked.

Locking the front door doesn't help much when the back door is left open. Whether viewed from a security or compliance perspective, the weakest link vulnerability must be managed as a requirement. Partial database SRC programs result in a false sense of protection and leave organizations out of compliance and vulnerable to attack.

With collapsing budgets and short project timelines, even the most diligent organizations may be challenged to lock down *all* their database environments. But information assurance professionals need not conclude that all hope is lost. Systems and processes not only exist to manage the challenge—they are also affordable and can be implemented in relatively short periods of time.

Chapter 4

ENEMY TACTICS

"Eighty-five percent of attacks [in 2009]
were not considered highly difficult. "[xliii]

Buffer Overflows, Denial of Service, and the SQL Slammer Worm

"Virus-Like Attack Hits Web Traffic," was the BBC News World Edition headline. The article declared "An attack by fast-spreading malicious code targeting computer servers has dramatically slowed Internet traffic...In South Korea Internet services were shut down nationwide for hours on Saturday... The nationwide Internet shutdown was triggered by 'apparent cyber terror committed by hackers,' the country's Yonhap news agency reported." [xliv]

On January 25, 2003 the world experienced one of the largest Denial of Service (DoS) attacks in history as the SQL Slammer Worm was unleashed. The attack spread at light speed, and in as little as ten minutes infected as many as 75,000 database servers, slowing down Internet traffic worldwide. While commonly known as the "SQL Slammer Worm," this virus was not a SQL injection attack, and it did not even use the SQL language. Named after Microsoft SQL Server, the database platform against which it was targeted, the SQL Slammer Worm exploited a known bug in MS SQL Server for which a patch had been released six months earlier. While some companies surely had updated their MS SQL Server databases when the patch was released from Microsoft, many others had not. Regardless, the denial of service that followed impacted the entire Internet.

Like the tsunami following an earthquake, the ensuing denial of service impact was far more devastating than the original worm attack. The SQL Slammer Worm took advantage of a common software bug called a buffer overflow. When instructions are read into memory without the length of the string being checked by the program, buffers overflow and the program begins to overwrite itself. In this case, the SQL Slammer Worm instructed the infected machines to randomly select IP addresses and then send out more SQL Slammer Worms. Those databases, in turn, repeated the malicious instruction, and more and more databases became infected in an out of control, viral escalation. While only 75,000 MS SQL Server databases were actually infected, millions more were indirectly impacted as the traffic created by the attack shut down data centers across the Internet, including at least one large bank whose ATM network was knocked offline for nearly two days. [xlv]

Internet monitoring sites such as Akamai and the Internet Storm Center documented dramatic slowdowns in global Internet traffic as the worm doubled every ten seconds. Nothing this catastrophic had happened since the Code Red Worm in 2001. Nearly all vulnerable databases were infected within ten minutes, and it took days to restore global Internet traffic to normal. [xlvi]

The SQL Slammer Worm was based on a paper presented at the Black Hat briefings by David Litchfield, a leading database security researcher. Generally, researchers only release such information to the general public after a patch has been released by the publisher of the vulnerable software. In this case, a patch had been available from Microsoft for six months prior to the worm's launch, but many organizations had failed to patch their databases.

In February 2010, Litchfield announced yet another critical vulnerability. Now known as the "Oracle-Litchfield Zero Day," Litchfield identified a Java vulnerability that allows a user to take over the database (and even the host) through privilege escalation. This particular vulnerability was estimated to affect nine out of ten Oracle databases worldwide, and this time the paper was presented *before* a patch was released. Proactive database SRC teams scrambled to work with independent database security and research teams to lock down their vulnerable databases and apply necessary fixes.

Privilege Escalation and Abuse

It would be an easy cure to simply revoke any user privileges that are excessive or pose a risk, but the truth is that someone must be in a position of absolute authority to govern and administer a database system. As a result, database administrators are frequently granted universal access and control of the database, and this role is called a privileged user. Best practices would suggest that such powerful system access only be granted through a formal attestation process and entitlement review. However, many organizations lack such control processes.

Database administrators hold exceptional power. Not only can they access any and all data in the system, they can also create new user profiles, amend the access rights of existing users, and control all activity regarding the disposition of the data. In some cases, the database administrator can even override the native audit and monitoring systems in the database. Once armed with the capability to turn off these audit controls, the DBA is, in theory, able to circumvent any and all forensic means of tracking database activity—meaning no fingerprints or footprints are left behind after malicious acts are committed.

Of course, database administrators are not the enemy. These individuals possess the critical skill set to make sure our databases perform well, and they represent an indispensable role in database SRC. The database administrator role is vital and must be protected. In fact, most cases of privilege abuse stem not from authorized database administrators, but from other users whose privileges have been escalated *outside* of any control process.

In one possible scenario, an unauthorized user may leverage a usage grant to "public" to gain authorized access, and then exploit any number of known configuration vulnerabilities to escalate their privileges to administrator status. In another scenario privilege escalations may occur without any malicious intent at all. Through role inheritance, which can occur almost naturally over periods of time, user privileges may unwittingly achieve elevated or even super user status.

Unintended privilege escalations are the result of weak access controls, and bad behavior is more likely when robust processes for database user entitlement are absent. SC Magazine reported in March 2009 that a Los Angeles area hospital recently fired fifteen workers and suspended eight others for accessing the medical records of octuplet mother Nadia Suleman without her permission. "Octomom" became a media sensation after giving birth to her octuplets in January 2009. Hospital officials told the *Los Angeles Times* that the breach was discovered through monitoring. The good news is the hospital was able to determine which employees had accessed Suleman's files. While kudos are due to the hospital database SRC team for discovering and reporting the HIPAA breach, everyone agrees that the hospital would have been better off if the breach had never occurred in the first place. If an entitlement review process had discovered the excessive user privileges, the hospital SRC team may have prevented the user entitlement violation before it ever occurred. [xlvii]

Whether privilege escalation occurs surreptitiously or through weak entitlement controls, hackers seek any number of ways to abuse and exploit this critical database vulnerability. Once privileged status is achieved, a hacker is able to take control of the database and wield enormous power over the sensitive information. If only to protect the innocent from being wrongfully accused, excessive privileges must be revoked, and compensating controls must be put in place to monitor privileged user activity.

Password Attacks

Even with proper security measures in place, sensitive information in a database is only as secure as the password required to gain access. Whether or not the target database is directly facing the Internet, or resides behind firewalls on a "super secure" network, bad guys who are also authorized users have potential access to sensitive information. With valid credentials the attacker is able to operate from within, and once the enemy is inside the camp, protection measures are more complicated and require alternative defense strategies.

Most organizations maintain tough password policies, and CISO teams tasked with enforcement must maintain their resolve in the face of user pushback. Users often feel harassed as they struggle to manage complex logon credentials, and they create their own methods to remember passwords. Two factor or multi-factor authentication approaches are often not considered practical. Identity management systems offer some relief, but they are difficult to implement and maintain, and they lack user entitlement management at the database level. The days of quick and easy passwords that never change are long gone as most organizations maintain password strength standards (for example, a minimum of eight alphanumeric characters with upper and lower case). With password changes required every few weeks, and no repeats allowed, users soon run out of ideas to create memorable passwords. Ultimately, they submit to the CISO controls and relent to the challenge of trying to remember and manage arcane character constructions that are only relevant as a valid user ID and password.

But how do users manage and store their access credentials? Some write them on a piece of paper and stuff them in a drawer, tuck them in a wallet, or post them on a pin cushion over their workstation. Others store them on their personal digital assistants (PDAs) often search indexed as "passwords." Sometimes the PDA requires yet another password to manage, and sometimes the PDA has no password protection at all. No matter how users elect to store their passwords, they must be written down in order to be remembered. Once written down, these passwords, no matter how strong, are vulnerable to discovery by the wrong person.

As authorized access is the easiest way into a database, hackers seek valid password accounts as a first choice to attain access. By simply rifling through drawers at work or by stealing an unlocked PDA, valid passwords are not difficult to find. More sophisticated password theft may involve social engineering, email phishing, key logging software, monitoring and surveillance of unencrypted network traffic, or the use of widely available brute force tools that try to guess weak passwords by attempting logon combinations over and over until valid access is found. In other words, there is no shortage of techniques available to procure authorized user credentials.

Default passwords represent a very different, but in some ways even more prolific attack vector. As opposed to account credentials that are stolen or used illegally, default passwords are valid account credentials that either are shipped with the shrink-wrapped database software or are established through the installation of application software that requires account access to the database. Security best practices recommend that all default passwords be changed by system administrators before production use, but database software ships with many default passwords. Perhaps the most famous authorized Oracle database user of all time is Logon ID "Scott" and Password "Tiger." Default accounts that ship with each version of every database are easily found online by using your favorite Internet search engine. Many default passwords ship locked by the database publisher, but unless default passwords are dutifully changed as required by best practices, anonymous access to the database may be available to anyone who has been introduced to "Scott / Tiger."

A database is only as secure as the Logon ID and password required for access, and "super secure" networks and perimeter defenses cannot defend against malicious users who are also authorized users. Considered by many as the most fundamental database attack vector of all, passwords represent critical database vulnerabilities, and database SRC teams must focus on strengthening their password defenses.

SQL Injection

For Albert Gonzalez and his band of criminal hackers, the target was the database, and the attack vector of choice was SQL injection. Like a vault to a bank robber, database systems lured Gonzalez because that's where the treasure was stored. Throughout his many campaigns, Gonzalez sought to first gain access to the database to retrieve the sensitive information, and then to sell the valuable data on the eastern European black market. Payments were typically laundered through wire service providers, and few tracks were left behind. While Gonzalez also used many other techniques (such as packet sniffing) to crack database security systems, SQL injection was a preferred tactic.

SQL or "Structured Query Language" is the programming command language by which programmers manipulate data in a relational database. Using a SQL injection attack, hackers seek to exploit Web application vulnerabilities in order to gain access to the database. There are many types of SQL injection attacks, but the basic approach is to entice a Web application to fail to process data inputs properly. Incorrectly filtered inputs into the Web application can create SQL calls that enable the hacker to inject payloads of malicious or malformed SQL commands into the database. Once a skilled attacker is able to communicate directly with the database, numerous exploits are possible.

Since the days of Albert Gonzalez, SQL injection has grown dramatically to become one of the most heavily used attack vectors. According to IBM ISS X-Force research,[xlviii] the number of daily SQL injections jumped by 50 percent from Q4 of 2008 to Q1 of 2009, then nearly doubled during Q2 of 2009. "Mass SQL injection" techniques that use hacking robots to inflict harm across much larger target areas are also on the rise. Through a "mass SQL injection attack" malicious code is injected into a Web application, which then connects to a database and other Web applications.[xlix] The malicious code then executes instructions to repeat the procedure and attack another database... and so on. With viral efficiency, the attack passes from one database to another.

Anatomy of a SQL Injection Attack

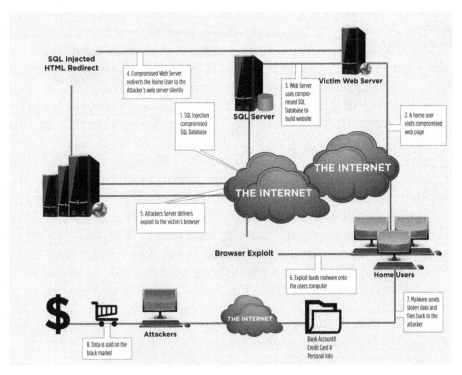

Figure 12: Anatomy of a SQL injection attack.

"In data breach scenarios, SQL injection has three main uses:

- Query the data from the database
- Modify data within the database
- Deliver malware to the system

The versatility and effectiveness of SQL injection make it a multi-tool of choice among cybercriminals."[l]

In January 2008 a "mass SQL injection" attack variant impacted over seventy thousand Websites. The attack targeted the Microsoft SQL Server database by placing malware inside the database tables. Once users connected to the database, their PC became infected with a nasty virus. Users had no way to defend themselves. This particular SQL injection attack targeted a fifteen-month-old Microsoft SQL Server vulnerability within Microsoft Data Access Components (MDAC) for which a patch had been released by Microsoft fifteen months earlier. Even though the application of a simple patch could have prevented the entire disaster, many thousands of databases were left vulnerable because too many database administrators did not follow best practices and stay current with critical patch levels.[li]

The cost of a SQL injection breach can be significant. In 2010, the brokerage firm Davidson & Co. was fined $375,000 by the Financial Industry Regulatory Authority (FINRA) after being victimized by a SQL injection attack. "Broker-dealers must be especially vigilant about protecting their customers' confidential information, which includes ensuring that their technology is sufficient," said James Shorris, Executive Vice President and Executive Director of enforcement for FINRA. The firm "failed to implement basic safeguards to protect their data—even though the firm had been advised before this incident to implement an intrusion detection system." In this case the firm had put no database security controls in place whatsoever. Not only did the attack exploit a weak password, which might have been revealed by vulnerability management scans, a lack of automated database activity monitoring meant that the logs were not routinely checked and the intrusion was not alerted as soon as it occurred. [lii]

Defense against a SQL injection attack requires a multi-layered approach, and protective measures should be architected with an end-to-end view. In other words, both the Web application and the database infrastructure must be included into the solution scope. Application-side vulnerability scanning of source code and Web server configurations as well as Web application firewalls (WAF) should be deployed to protect Internet facing applications. Such security best practices limit the attack surface of the application by ensuring secure coding standards, identifying configuration vulnerabilities, and monitoring SQL traffic for attacks.

But, as an equally important measure, we must take steps to protect the database as well, because risks still remain. Battles to defend against attacks are continuously raging, and each side is constantly escalating. As soon as the attackers find a new chink in the armor (such as a vulnerable Web application), CISO teams deploy counter measures. But then, not a moment later, new attacks are launched for which attack signatures are not yet identified. Subsequently, when the WAF fails to recognize an attack signature and allows an attack through, database activity monitoring solutions become a last line of defense. Database activity monitoring solutions can monitor the attack as it happens, fire alerts, and prevent any real problems or lasting damage. In cyber war, the advantage is always to the bad guys because the attackers are always one step ahead. [liii]

While application-side defenses are necessary, by themselves they are not sufficient. This means database-specific protection measures must be in place as well. End-to-end protection is required, and DBA teams must be armed with the capability to identify database vulnerabilities and the tools to monitor *how* and *when* the application is accessing the database. Despite the availability of source code and Web server scanning programs, vulnerabilities remain in many production applications, leaving the database vulnerable. Moreover, simple awareness of database configuration vulnerabilities and patch gaps are not enough. As the Davidson breach clearly demonstrates, database patches must be applied and configuration vulnerabilities must be remediated in order to protect sensitive data.

Effective defense against SQL injection is possible only when database protections are put in place alongside Web application defenses. Database SRC teams who follow best practices to manage vulnerabilities such as misconfigurations and weak passwords are able to reduce the risk of a successful SQL injection attack to near zero. In addition, database SRC teams who leverage database activity monitoring and provide regular forensic analysis of logs can successfully manage the threat of future attacks from occurring. [liv]

Today, SQL injection is the number one threat to sensitive data, accounting for nearly one-fifth of all security breaches (19 percent). [lv] But we needn't despair since the good news is this: effective defense strategies exist, and they can be readily deployed. The critical element is that security solutions must be deployed end-to-end, beyond just the application tier. A second line of defense is required to protect the database itself because that's where sensitive data resides nearly all the time. Mitchell Harper, cofounder of e-commerce firm *BigCommerce*, writes, "The database is the heart of most Web applications: it stores the data needed for the websites and applications to survive." [lvi]

Chapter 5

USER RIGHTS

*"If you had unprecedented access 14 hours a day 7 days
a week for 8+ months, what would you do?"*
–Private First Class Bradley Manning [lvii]

Employee Anonymity and Toxic Combinations

For large institutions, rapid organizational change and growth leads to greater and greater employee anonymity as individuals fade into the masses. Such anonymity can conceal the actions of malicious hackers and challenge modern security controls.

Professor M. Eric Johnson at the Tuck School of Business at Dartmouth studied how organizational complexity creates security challenges. From field research conducted while embedded in the security teams at several large banking institutions, he found that these financial services companies offer a "vivid example" of access control complexity as these firms merge and consolidate to create massive collections of people organized globally into hundreds of functional domains. [lviii]

As financial services firms operating large-scale, complex systems struggle to configure the right levels of data access and to restrict access to sensitive and privileged information, Johnson describes "a toxic combination" where weak system access controls may allow users "to break the law, violate rules of ethics, damage customers' trust, or even just create the appearance of impropriety." [lix]

Johnson cites the following sobering example:

> There are many ways for toxic combinations to occur. Sometimes it is a mistake of not terminating access following a promotion or transfer; other times it is a fault of entitlement design. An example of toxic combinations occurring from a promotion could be as seemingly innocuous as an accounts payable clerk retaining the

access to write checks once they have been promoted so they can fill in at busy times, while their new job allows them to go back to edit and even delete check writing records—in essence giving them the opportunity to steal money. A design flaw example would be a trader in a commercial bank having access to see holdings of the accounts for clients he manages, as well as those of other traders' clients. The trader's access could be used to counter the aggressive positions of his non-direct client to the enriching of himself and others, which is not only unethical, but highly illegal. [ix]

Again it is massive complexity which creates the "toxic combinations" which Professor Johnson describes. Large institutions such as the banks which he studied may have hundreds of thousands of employees requiring unique entitlement profiles to data residing in tens of thousands of databases. Complicating the task further is the significant list of entitlements from which to choose to enable an individual user to properly perform their job. Too few entitlements may impact worker productivity. Too many may increase the likelihood of cyber attack and audit failure.

Separation of Duty and the Principle of Least Privilege

In the post-Enron world, requirements for internal controls have emerged and evolved into audited compliance frameworks, and public entities have adopted comprehensive risk management models such as COBIT and COSO in response to Section 404 of the Sarbanes-Oxley Act. Separation of duty and the principle of least privilege are cornerstones of these frameworks, and organizations, large ones in particular, are challenged to manage and implement sensitive data access controls as a fundamental compliance requirement.

While common sense dictates that "the fox should not be left to watch the henhouse," compliance to such a simple concept is a major challenge. In the database world this is true for even the most sophisticated organizations. End users require access to database applications to perform their jobs. The more job responsibility they receive, the greater level of access privilege they require. The greater level of access privilege they are granted, the less control organizations are able to exercise.

This reality raises three questions:

- How much business risk is acceptable for a given degree of access privilege?

- What controls are appropriate to govern access to different types of sensitive data?

- What level of privilege should be granted to what types of sensitive data?

To manage these access control challenges, audit firms recommend the principle of least privilege, which suggests that employees be entitled to only the minimum level of access to the database as required for properly performing their job. In theory, the principle of least privilege makes perfect sense. But once again, the devil is in the details in as much as database utilities lack appropriate reporting tools to manage least privilege implementations. As a result, least privilege entitlement reviews and implementations can be complex and time-consuming in the absence of database SRC solution capabilities. In fact, manual entitlement review of a typical database can exceed eighty man-hours.

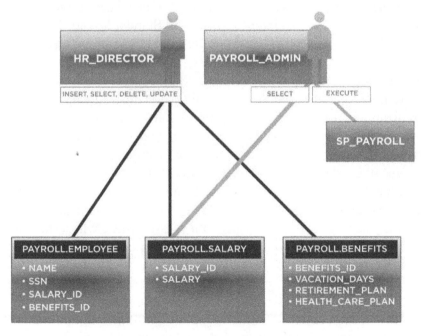

Figure 13: The complexities of mapping database users to groups, roles, and permissions.

US Army Private First Class Bradley Manning became the poster child for the theory of least privilege when it was revealed that somehow he had downloaded over 250 thousand classified US Department of Defense and US State Department documents and cables and handed them over to truth activist and Wikileaks founder Julian Assange.

"If you had unprecedented access 14 hours a day 7 days a week for 8+ months, what would you do?" PFC Manning asked.[lxi]

Why a low level US Army intelligence analyst possessed such broad access to classified information is not only an important policy question, it is also an important operational issue. While the investigation of the Wikileaks breach is still underway, we can be certain that data protection policies will be found to have been circumvented. But perhaps more profound, we are likely to learn that the operational processes for attestation of user rights either did not exist or were not being properly executed.

Role-Based Access Control and Inheritance

Role-Based Access Control (RBAC) has been established by bodies such as The National Institute of Standards and Technology (NIST)[lxii] to assist security professionals and DBAs in the management and assignment of access controls, user rights, and privileges. Database technology providers employ RBAC systems, but real world experience proves that such tools are insufficient for most organizations. The problems begin as soon as the initial entitlement review of access privileges is complete, and the natural fluidity of movement begins to occur within an organization.

In the database world, entitlement review involves the assignment of roles to users that, in turn, defines access controls and privileges such as SELECT, INSERT, UPDATE, DELETE, or DENY. Generally, CISO and DBA organizations are tasked with establishing and deploying RBAC policy based on the concepts of least privilege and separation of duty.

Let's assume that as part of the initial entitlement review process, the CISO team designs two HR department roles as follows:

This design calls for a clear separation of duties to be established with access granted according to the principle of least privilege. The HR_ADMIN privileges should be restricted to only read (SELECT) salary information and run (EXECUTE) the payroll process, whereas the HR_DIRECTOR carries read, write, and modify (SELECT, INSERT, UPDATE, and DELETE) on all employee data. Note that the design calls for the ADMIN to have a privilege the DIRECTOR does not have (i. e., to run the payroll.) This subtle restriction in the design is intended to address a possible toxic combination of privileges, where the HR_DIRECTOR could easily create a new employee, run payroll to pay them, and then delete the employee from the system. This would allow the HR_DIRECTOR to steal from his or her employer. While well-conceived in the design phase, in this case the initial entitlement did not include proper documentation, setting the stage for a privilege escalation to create an unintended separation of duty violation.

The design is approved, and then handed off to the database engineering and operations team for implementation. A DBA is assigned to provision the database access. Before getting started, the DBA examines the project requirements as well as the company org chart and learns that the HR_ADMIN is a direct report to the HR_DIRECTOR. With a full understanding of the assigned project to update the HR system, the DBA begins the exercise of provisioning database access.

The plan is to utilize the RBAC system built into the database. Roles will be created for each job function, privileges will be assigned to each role, and then employees will be added to the roles. Since privileges are managed at the role, rather than at the user level, this best practices plan will make it easy to make future changes as the organization grows and changes.

The DBA begins by creating two new database roles: HR_DIRECTOR and HR_ADMIN. The DBA then moves to provision the HR_ADMIN, granting the role SELECT on the SALARY table, and EXECUTE on the SP_PAYROLL function. Next, the DBA moves on to the HR_DIRECTOR. Knowing that the HR administrators report directly to the HR director, the first step is to make the HR_DIRECTOR role a member of the HR_ADMIN role. The DBA then adds the additional privileges to the HR_DIRECTOR, granting SELECT, INSERT, UPDATE, and DELETE privileges on the EMPLOYEE, SALARY, and BENEFITS tables. Finally, the DBA grants role membership to the appropriate user accounts, making three people in the HR department members of HR_ADMIN. Their manager is granted role membership to the HR_DIRECTOR role. Feeling satisfied with a well-thought-out implementation, the DBA reports the project as completed and moves on to other work.

Many months pass before a segregation of duties audit is performed on the HR function of this organization. During that time, the DBA who originally provisioned the system left the company. Everyone was surprised when the auditors presented the organization with a high severity audit finding stating that proper controls are not in place to prevent stealing from the organization by creating phantom employees and paying them.

A new DBA is assigned to analyze and fix the situation. The first analysis shows nothing wrong. The right HR employees are provisioned and appear to be assigned to the proper roles. Further analyzing the roles, neither the HR_ADMIN nor HR_DIRECTOR appears to have more rights than the original design dictated. As the hours and days pass, the urgency to close the audit finding grows. Testing is performed to validate the finding, and it becomes clear that the HR_DIRECTOR can indeed create employees, pay them, and then remove them from the system.

How did this happen?

Role inheritance is the culprit. At some point in the process, perhaps when one of the payroll administrators was absent, sick, or on vacation, the DBA set the HR_DIRECTOR to inherit the role of HR_ADMIN, so he or she could perform the job of the absent employee. Since the administrators all report to the director, it seemed like a logical decision. However, this change indirectly granted the HR_DIRECTOR the privilege to EXECUTE the payroll function. When the admin returned to work, the undocumented inheritance was never reversed.

Such an occurrence is only one example of the "toxic combination" of privileges that the initial entitlement review process was constructed to avoid. Role inheritance is rarely documented properly, and RBAC systems built into the database as utilities are unable to report on such conflicts, making such a separation of duty violation nearly impossible to detect without a separate and distinct database entitlement management system. Even more frustrating, the initial entitlement review established separation of duty and least privilege properly. Despite the attestation process of initial and subsequent entitlement review, and without malicious intent, the separation of duty control violation still occurred.

Separation of Duty and Least Privilege

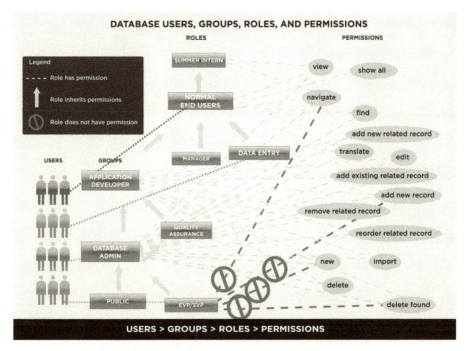

Figure 14: Defined by the Clark Wilson Integrity Model, Separation of Duty is the principal that requires that the certifier and the implementer of an action be different entities.[lxiii]

Excessive privileges caused by inherited roles can easily become lost in the complexity of a database RBAC system. Verizon reports, "In general, we find that employees are granted more privileges than they need to perform their job duties, and the activities that do require higher privileges are usually not monitored in any real way."[lxiv] Organizations must put proactive measures in place to prevent this occurrence and take steps based in best practice for proper access control to sensitive information. One solution is to implement a user rights management system. Why wait for an audit finding or forensic crime report to discover such a "toxic combination"?

Chapter 6

DEFENSIVE STRATEGY

"Ninety-six percent of breaches were avoidable through simple or intermediate controls." [lxv]

Database SRC Starts with the Scan

Before undertaking a critical medical procedure such as an operation, doctors first focus on making a correct diagnosis. MRI and CAT scans are essential tools in the field of medical diagnostics because they are non-invasive, fast, easy to administer, relatively lowcost, and they provide *immediate* results. For these same reasons database SRC programs should always start with a vulnerability scan (an MRI of your database, metaphorically speaking).

Because they can be deployed quickly and with minimal project effort, database vulnerability scans offer immediate time-to-benefit. As a critical control process, scanning begins to deliver value on an enterprise-wide scale as soon as it is implemented. But even more importantly, scanning offers a proactive approach to database SRC by providing critical information such as answers to the following questions:

- What is the database asset inventory?
- Which databases house sensitive data?
- What access controls are in place?
- What vulnerabilities exist?
- What remediation steps should be taken?

The stakes are high in database security, yet simple solutions exist that are easy to implement. Scanning technology establishes a program of proactive threat management and demonstrates compliance control. Armed proactively with critical discovery and vulnerability information, database SRC teams are able to prioritize fixes and make better decisions because they have full visibility of the remediation requirements.

Sometimes the list of database vulnerabilities revealed by a scan includes threats that are already planned for remediation at a later time, or cannot be remediated at all. In such cases, SRC best practice dictates that these vulnerabilities be monitored to establish a compensating control. For example, if we understand that privileged users represent a possible separation of duty compliance gap, we must also appreciate that it is not possible to remove all privileged users from a database. So, we must therefore monitor privileged users, but must we monitor *all* privileged users on *all* databases?

First, let us ask a more basic question: Who are the privileged users anyway? Are privileged users only those users assigned to a specific privileged role called "database administrator"? Or is a privileged user more accurately defined as any user whose privileges are excessive to his or her job role? Let's remember that to satisfy the audit finding, we have two choices: we must either resolve the separation of duty condition or implement monitoring as a compensating control.

It stands to reason that fixing vulnerabilities is preferable to implementing and managing an ongoing compensating control such as database activity monitoring. The preferred approach to managing privileged users, therefore, is to first scan all user entitlements to determine a baseline of the existing privilege assignments. Next, an entitlement review process should be run to establish desired user rights based on least privilege. Finally, the entitlement review process should provide attestation for all users, especially those users who will be granted privileged account status. Once a list of authorized privileged users is established, the excessive privileges of all other users should be revoked. In this way the monitoring scope is reduced and becomes more manageable. A database vulnerability and user rights scan not only establishes a higher level of protection, it also helps filter the monitoring scope and reduce performance overhead. When database SRC starts with a scan, organizations save time, expenses, and computing resources.

The Agentless Manifesto

As organizations establish programs for database SRC, the ability to scale control processes across the enterprise quickly emerges as a number one success factor. But scaling infrastructure projects enterprise wide can challenge even the most steadfast IT teams. A database is only as secure as its weakest link, and organizations realize that project scopes must include all databases across the enterprise to deliver security and compliance controls that are complete. Again, just as it makes no sense to lock the front door and leave the back door open, organizations must not only lock down critical databases (such as SOX-designated instances), but also non-critical database instances where database links offer back door access to sensitive information.

For smaller companies with fewer database instances to protect, IT resources are still scarce, so any project must scale fast through implementation and be easy to manage and service down the road. Large organizations managing thousands of database instances are concerned over partial deployment outcomes, performance impacts on mission-critical systems, and the complexity of managing thousands of endpoints. Most CIO's, having learned hard lessons through other challenging enterprise-wide deployments, seek assurance that successful project outcomes will be achieved on time and within budget. Project success is often recognized by the quickest time-to-value, the lowest total cost of ownership (TCO), and the most rapid return on investment (ROI).

Agentless architectures are defined as software deployments where no foreign or third-party software is installed on the endpoint locations, or in the case of database SRC, installed on the database hosts. Such architectures are intrinsically more scalable, manageable, and serviceable as the entire solution can be deployed on the smallest possible footprint, such as a single server. Agentless architectures do not require multiple database SRC appliances to achieve security and compliance results. Agentless deployments enable enterprise-wide scopes to be brought live in the shortest possible timeframes and with smaller teams. Furthermore, agentless deployments mean security and compliance controls start delivering value as soon as the go-live deployment occurs. Total cost of ownership (TCO) and return on investment (ROI) advantages are obvious, since SRC project teams only need to manage a single software deployment as opposed to tens, hundreds, or even thousands of individual agents.

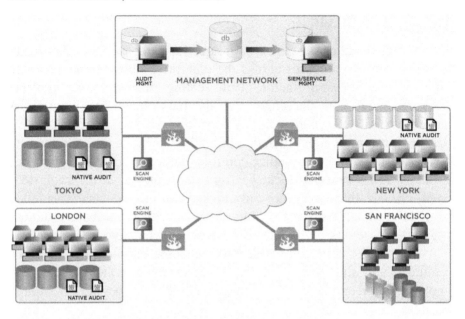

Figure 15: Agentless database SRC architecture.

Database scanning is an agentless architecture which features a light-weight infrastructure footprint reducing the cost and complexity of implementation. The impact of agentless scanning on mission critical systems is low because no foreign software is installed or maintained. DBAs benefit from less risk to database performance and reduced maintenance requirements.

Agent-based approaches, on the other hand, require the deployment and management of foreign software over the long term. Such architectures require not only one-off installation, but also ongoing maintenance, patch management, and performance tuning to minimize the impact on production systems. By way of example, most database activity monitoring (DAM) solutions require the installation of software agents either on the database host itself, or on the network supporting the database. As we have discussed, while quite effective at monitoring SQL traffic, these agents also generate network and database activity of their own. If not managed closely, such overhead can impact database and network performance. Consequently, DAM solutions must be deployed and managed carefully so they are able to scale across the enterprise.

To manage the performance concerns of DAM deployments, and to help them scale, database administrators seek to filter and minimize the monitoring scope. No matter if the monitoring activity is host or network based, less monitoring means less network traffic and less data to manage overall. Vulnerability scanning provides the intelligence needed to effectively filter and target database activity monitoring scopes. Through an agentless vulnerability scan conducted upstream from the monitoring process, known threats can be identified and remediated proactively. By filtering and reducing the scope of monitoring, vulnerability scanning is able to reduce the cost and complexity of enterprise database activity monitoring.

For most organizations, the forensic audit capabilities of DAM are a necessary requirement and important compensating control for known vulnerabilities such as privileged users. Well-architected and properly deployed DAM systems may also offer real time intrusion detection systems (IDS). But why operate in reactive mode at all? Why wait for a breach or control violation to occur, only to report about it after the fact? Doesn't it make more sense to identify and remediate threats in the first place?

Database SRC starts with an agentless scan because it enables proactive remediation of vulnerabilities and reduces monitoring scope. As opposed to more intrusive agent-based approaches, agentless architectures provide DBA stakeholders improved stability and serviceability over mission-critical systems. Database applications may be upgraded and patched regardless of foreign agent dependencies, and organizations are better able to service their critical applications. This operational autonomy not only improves reliability, availability, and serviceability, it represents best practice for the management of mission-critical applications.

Database SRC Life Cycle Best Practices

Best practices are all about *completeness*. Scanning, monitoring, and data encryption—while necessary and critical elements of a best practice approach—are, by themselves, only table-stake capabilities, and they are insufficient when deployed separately or alone. All tier one database platforms today offer data encryption capabilities as a built-in feature. Whether encryption is implemented while data is "at rest" or "in motion" is the function of an effective policy management program. As with securing other critical infrastructure elements, organizations seeking to achieve best practice in database SRC should commit to a full life cycle approach to achieve truly reliable protection. The database SRC lifecycle is a continuous program that involves an iterative process of discovery, policy management, vulnerability assessment, user entitlement review, prioritization of fixes, remediation, monitoring of known vulnerabilities, and finally, deep reporting and analytics of the entire life cycle.

Practitioners generally agree on the following six phase best practices approach to manage the database SRC life cycle:

Figure 16: The database SRC life cycle best practice methodology.

Discover: Create and describe the database asset inventory. Where are the databases located? What kind of databases are they? Who owns each database, and who is responsible for managing them? Which databases store sensitive data? What types of sensitive data are in the inventory?

Classify: Establish classifications for corporate data. Catalogue and develop a baseline to manage database assets through policies for protection. Set appropriate rules and controls for managing sensitive data. Establish and document the database SRC plan.

Assess: Identify all vulnerabilities which are present according to protection policies. Review user rights and data access profiles. Determine password strengths and weaknesses. Are the database configurations secured against known vulnerabilities? Have necessary patches been applied?

Prioritize: Based on assessment data and asset classification, segment vulnerabilities into high, medium, and low priority. Establish ongoing plans for remediation.

Fix: Execute remediation tasks against the prioritized list of vulnerabilities. Strengthen passwords, revoke excessive privileges, fix configurations, and close patch gaps.

Monitor: Monitor all known vulnerabilities such as privileged user activity, and watch un-patched systems. Alert on suspicious or malicious activity.

Report: Create evidentiary reporting and audit trails to establish an SRC profile of the database inventory. Prepare specific reporting to satisfy individual compliance guidelines such as SOX and PCI DSS.

For completeness, database SRC best practices must include all phases of the life cycle, and the process must be iterative. Completeness means assessment targets must be derived from a thorough discovery process, and monitoring rules must be based on documented policies. And because the database asset inventory is continually evolving as new instances are added, updated, and deleted at any moment, the best practice life cycle must be executed iteratively and on an ongoing basis.

Continuous Compliance

Today's business operates in a compliance driven regulatory environment, and IT organizations have learned that successful auditor/enterprise relationships require adherence to compliance regulations. Fortunately, many of the best practices that organizations deploy to achieve database security also reduce corporate risk and improve database compliance. What's more, database security grounds compliance where the data lives—in the database.

However, organizations often operate in reactive mode, awaiting the discovery of a control violation or an audit finding before taking action. As soon as the audit finding has unleashed chaos and gained management attention, the organization scrambles teams to close the gap. While such a reactive approach may deliver results after the fact, it also increases the cost of compliance and is disruptive to the organization. The obvious question is this: Why aren't organizations more proactive? Why wait to learn that the databases are not only out of compliance, but also unprotected? Shouldn't we take proactive steps to avoid the train wreck, as opposed to scrambling first responder teams to pick up the pieces?

The goal must be to establish a control framework offering continuous compliance. Continuous compliance implies an inherently disciplined system based on best practices where documented controls, policy driven processes, reporting, and ongoing improvements are a standard operating procedure. In such an environment, organizations have established a framework of proactive measures that offers the best possible means of prevention. But since we recognize that no security system is impenetrable, continuous compliance enables organizations to master the basic control processes required to flag violations and intrinsically answer the four most basic forensic questions:

- What happened?
- How did it happen?
- Who did it?
- When did they do it?

In addition to being persistent and able to demonstrate compliance on demand, a system of continuous compliance must be proactive. Rather than allow an audit to unleash chaos, organizations have a significant opportunity to operate more productively and with less disruption. By establishing a proactive control framework, continuous compliance reduces corporate risk overall.

In a continuous compliance environment the audit focus moves away from the SRC status of a single database instance and towards the effectiveness of the database SRC control program overall. Rather than drilling into the rights management status of a particular database or the compensating controls placed over certain privileged users, the audit objective is primarily to determine if the database SRC control program is deployed properly and operating as intended.

When an audit finds that an enterprise-wide database SRC control process not only exists, but is properly deployed and working, organizations gain assurance that their sensitive data is secure and compliant. In the absence of a continuous compliance program, auditors must establish the state of compliance through a "point-and-shoot" approach. The "point-and-shoot" approach means that IT auditors may select any single database, even at random, to perform a database SRC audit. With so many regulations requiring control process attestation, and with so many database servers to manage, such a scenario leaves the database SRC team totally reactive and near defenseless. Continuous compliance, on the other hand, means auditors abandon the "point-and-shoot" approach and turn their attention to the effectiveness of the database SRC control process as a whole.

A Single Version of the Truth

With the audit scope now centered on the control process as opposed to the audit of a random database instance, our ability to slice and dice database SRC information from across the enterprise and deliver it on demand becomes a critical capability. Database SRC is all about effective reporting, and continuous compliance requires a single version of the truth.

"What is the database asset inventory?" "Where is sensitive data located?" "Which users have access to sensitive data?" "What database vulnerabilities exist this month versus last?" "What policies govern each database?" The operational processes of database SRC are driven by effective reporting as DBA, CISO and risk management teams work cross functionally to secure the enterprise and establish compliance.

Data warehouse functionality thus becomes a critical capability as pertinent information is continually being collected throughout the database SRC lifecycle, and the volume of data collected can become immense. Under a continuous compliance model, auditors seek to understand not only if essential processes exist, but also if these processes are being followed. The data warehouse approach supports these critical audit concerns by providing a broad spectrum of reporting across the entire enterprise scope of databases. By managing and storing the evidentiary foundation of the audit, the data warehouse establishes a single version of the truth for database SRC across the enterprise.

Chapter 7

THE DATABASE SRC PLATFORM

"In 2009, targeted attacks accounted for 89 percent of records compromised." [lxvi]

Enterprise Solution Architecture

To achieve continuous compliance, database SRC requires enterprise solution architecture. Cross-platform management from a single console is a key requirement as modern organizations maintain and operate mission-critical applications on operating systems and databases from several different suppliers. SRC teams must manage separate and distinct compliance policies assigned to each database instance. Oracle 10g database compliance policies are separate and distinct from the policies that govern Microsoft SQL Server 2008 R2, and the compliance demands of the HR department will be different from those of the finance department. It is impractical for database SRC teams to manage unique programs for every database publisher.

Therefore, a key question is: How does an organization govern the compliance requirements of so many heterogeneous database endpoints across the enterprise? Even more importantly, how does an organization provide reporting and a single version of the truth for database SRC? Database SRC requirements include not only a centralized management console, but a highly scalable, cross-platform solution architecture as well.

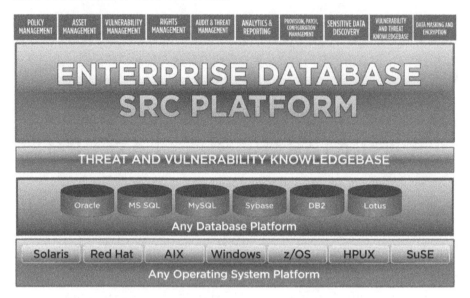

*Figure 17: The enterprise database SRC platform–support
for any operating system and any database.*

The solution architecture of an integrated set of database SRC applications should deliver a complete and comprehensive framework for risk management. Furthermore, the solution architecture must support the entire enterprise and deliver a single version of the truth. To support a best practices foundation, enterprise solution architectures offer broad platform support for tier-one operating systems (such as Linux, UNIX variations, and IBM z Series) as well as databases (such as IBM DB2, Oracle, Microsoft SQL Server, Sybase and MySQL).

But technical solution architecture alone is not enough. There are at least eleven integrated application areas that comprise database SRC. They are:

- Asset Management
- Sensitive Data Discovery
- Policy Management
- Vulnerability Management
- Threat Knowledge Base
- User Entitlement Management
- Configuration Management

- Data Masking
- Encryption
- Audit and Threat Management
- Analytics

Let's consider each integrated application area more closely.

Asset Management

In support of the initial discovery phase of the best practice database SRC lifecycle, the asset management application provides a complete inventory of all databases on the corporate network. Leveraging agentless, network-based scanning technology, asset management discovers and identifies every database on the network through "outside-in" penetration testing. Similar to a hacker perspective, the "outside-in" approach examines applications with essentially zero knowledge.

A typical pen test approach is used without any login credentials to answer the question, "What is it?" Penetration tests return fingerprint results that are referenced against a knowledgebase to discover key identification characteristics such as the specific database publisher, release detail, and the business unit owner. Based on these results, an asset inventory is created.

Producing a list of database assets may seem an academic exercise, but most organizations (especially large ones) do not have a reliable process of database inventory control. The creation of a database inventory baseline is the first step in developing an effective risk management program. The database SRC enterprise platform must help teams catalogue and control database inventory in an accurate and current state.

Database management is dynamic by nature. For every production instance of a database, it is not unusual to maintain three, six, or even a dozen nonproduction instances (used for development, testing, and training). Organizations create and decommission clones and subsets of production databases on a regular basis, resulting in constant changes to the database asset inventory. Access control and the management of sensitive information is especially challenging with respect to nonproduction instances. Organizations must concern themselves as much, if not more, with this particular threat. Database configurations and patch levels can become quickly obsolete as development and test teams iterate through the software development life cycle. As a result, the asset management process must be *continuous*.

Sensitive Data Discovery

The database asset inventory, while extremely necessary, is not sufficient on its own. Where is the sensitive data? Which databases maintain social security numbers, credit card information, or personal information? Which databases are simply processing the lunch menu or the corporate softball roster? In order to begin the process of data classification, the discovery process must also find and identify the sensitive data.

Not only a critical component of the asset management application, sensitive data discovery also serves other database SRC application domains, including data masking, encryption, data leak prevention (DLP), policy management, user rights management, and vulnerability assessment. All these database SRC applications must be completely aware of sensitive data. With potentially thousands of tables of data to review, manual discovery is simply not feasible. Therefore, automated discovery must not only be intelligent, it must be able to scale across as many database instances as necessary.

Sensitive data must be accurate, fully documented, and false positive identifications must be avoided. The discovery process must ultimately be "application aware" by being able to manage exception values, discrepancies, and derived values.

Policy Management

Armed with the baselines of database asset management and sensitive data discovery, the SRC team is now able to establish a policy management framework. Database SRC policies are established by a centralized template to configure the rules and control parameters of protection. Templates may follow standard definitions to support common compliance regulations (such as SOX and HIPAA), or organizations may edit or build custom database SRC policies based on internal standards. Once established, the policy management system forms the backbone of a risk management framework for continuous compliance.

Templates with preset permissions allow default policies to be quickly and easily configured for SOX, GLBA, DISA STIG, and other common compliance regulations. The ability to use pre-determined templates significantly reduces the manual effort required to create, review, test, publish, update, and track SRC policies. Administrators may also reconfigure and customize the templates. For example, penetration test security checks may include Brute Force or Denial of Service. Or, they may be set to Full, Safe, Heavy, Medium, or Light. Database applications with specific requirements may be configured with custom policies and permission sets. For example, if an application requires that access be granted to "PUBLIC," then permission sets may be deployed so that suspicious user-defined SQL statements such as SELECT*FROM USERS (select all values from the user table) either return no values, are alerted, or blocked.

The policy management application is the heart of the database SRC platform and automates the classification process in a consistent fashion. This comprehensive approach centralizes the process of creating and editing policies for data governance and allows organizations to maintain continuous compliance in an evolving regulatory environment. Out-of-the-box compliance knowledge means that the SRC team spends less time creating and more time enforcing the controls to be examined in the audit process. As a result SRC initiatives are accelerated, and total project costs are greatly reduced.

Vulnerability Assessment

Buffer overflows, password attacks, privilege escalations, and unauthorized operating system access—these are the vulnerabilities, attack signatures, and misconfiguration scenarios that constitute database threats. The vulnerability assessment application examines, reports, and proposes fixes for such security holes. Identified issues may include default or weak passwords, missing patches, poor access controls, and a host of other conditions. By establishing a vulnerability profile for each database in the enterprise, vulnerability assessment identifies the threats and compliance gaps for remediation.

Auditors choose between an outside-in, or "hacker's eye view", of the database (which requires no credentials), and/or a more thorough inside-out scan which requires read-only database account credentials. Vulnerability assessment is policy driven and identifies deltas and gaps between the current build of the database and the build specifications set forth in the protection policy. A vulnerability profile is created based on the security best practices of various regulatory compliance initiatives such as DISA STIG, NIST 800-53 (FISMA), PCI DSS, HIPAA, GLBA, Sarbanes-Oxley, ISO 17001/17799, COBIT, and Canada's MITS.

The vulnerability assessment application performs an *agentless* scan of the database settings, entitlements, passwords, and configurations. Policy driven checks are then run against a threat knowledge base to identify vulnerabilities, threats and audit exposures. The scan output comprises a list of vulnerabilities and threats prioritized by severity. Best-of-breed threat knowledge base solutions also include fix information. Armed with a database vulnerability profile that is regulatory specific, organizations are now able to demonstrate operational control.

Threat Knowledgebase

The threat knowledgebase is the key differentiator for a vulnerability assessment solution. If the knowledgebase is incomplete, or out of date, scans may be run and vulnerabilities will be missed. As a result, a vulnerability assessment solution is only as worthy as the research behind the discovery, definition, testing, and remediation of specific threats catalogued in the threat knowledgebase.

Database SRC threats are derived from research and include checks and rules pertaining to the secure and compliant implementation of a database. The threat knowledge base is the central reference and repository for all vulnerability and fix information. Database vulnerability scan results must be reference checked against the threat knowledgebase in order to flag a specific vulnerability. With so many database releases installed and in use, the challenge to provide a complete and current portfolio of known threat signatures, configuration vulnerabilities, and patch-level issues is enormous. Not only must the threat knowledgebase cover all the different database platforms (such as Microsoft, IBM, and Oracle), it also must cover the many different releases and patch sets currently in use.

With each new database release, the threat knowledgebase must be updated. Like a virus definition file, the threat knowledgebase changes constantly as ongoing research discovers new threats (like the 'Oracle-Litchfield Zero-Day"). With each new discovery, an update must be downloaded to keep the vulnerability assessment scans current against threats.

Database threat researchers seek to develop the fixes at the same time they develop the vulnerability checks. By researching and testing the fix ahead of time, threat researchers are able to save the DBA team significant time and effort. Such fixes should include appropriate documentation, describing not only the vulnerability, but also critical information regarding the fix, and its pre-tested implementation process. Threat research, therefore, is only complete when the vulnerability is discovered, documented, a check is created, and the fix is tested and proposed. All of this information is subsequently stored and managed in the threat knowledgebase.

Upon the discovery of new vulnerabilities, the threat knowledge base provides reference for the SRC team to make impact and severity assessments and prioritize remediation activity. The remediation is often to apply a fix in the form of a fix script. Fix scripts are SQL commands designed to correct misconfigurations and address the vulnerabilities identified by the scan. As DBA teams may spend a large portion of their time creating, testing, and applying fix scripts, automation of the process represents a tremendous opportunity to increase DBA productivity and drive value. By leveraging a continually updated and researched knowledgebase—which not only defines the specific threats and vulnerabilities, but also proposes pre-tested fixes—the DBAs can dramatically save time.

User Rights Management

Separation of duty is a cornerstone of not only every major compliance regulation, but also of sound security practice. This central database SRC principle seeks to prevent the aforementioned scenario of "the fox watching the hen house." Use cases may include any circumstance where individuals are granted excessive database access and privileges without proper attestation or a compensating control. For example, a payroll administrator should not be granted privilege to update his or her own salary field and then print a check. Similarly, an accounts payable clerk should not be granted privileges to both create and pay vendors. So how does the database SRC team establish such control processes?

User rights management helps organizations establish separation of duty control and provision user rights and entitlements according to the principle of least privilege across all enterprise databases. Today, when audit teams examine separation of duty as it applies to databases, the role of privileged users is generally a central focus. DBAs assigned privileged user accounts represent a classic separation of duty audit finding. Since the least privilege for a database administrator to perform their job equates to universal privileges across the database, there is no way to resolve the vulnerability. In such cases database activity monitoring (DAM) is often applied as a compensating control. But what if another user account, not intended to serve as a database administrator or super-user, has achieved excessive privileges through role inheritance? How would the database SRC team even know a problem exists if the only reporting available to them is the RBAC system that lacks the critical ability to detail such information on role inheritance?

Without an ongoing database rights review process, privilege escalation may go unnoticed. Real-time monitoring of all database user activity is a poor remedy because of overhead and performance concerns on the database and network. On the other hand, limits placed on the monitoring scope and configuration may mean that privileged activity goes undetected. So, how do we prevent this important control violation from proceeding unchecked? The database SRC team has only two choices: monitor or remediate. Remediation is always the first option, because eliminating the problem is preferable to the management of an ongoing compensating control through monitoring.

User rights management offers a comprehensive solution by providing reports on the privileges of each user as well as details into who has what type of access to sensitive data. Armed with this information, SRC teams are able to identify all assigned privileges that are excessive, including those that are inherited, and revoke them if necessary. Such an assessment process allows the database SRC team to maintain user rights as they were originally conceived during the initial entitlement review and to flag changes for attestation.

DATABASE USER RIGHTS MANAGEMENT

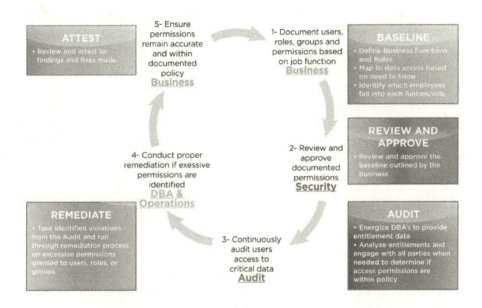

Figure 18: The database user rights management life cycle

Configuration Management

Whether a vulnerability assessment or user rights management scan reports a misconfiguration, patch gap, or privilege escalation, it is not sufficient to simply discover the threat. To avoid having to implement a compensating control, SRC teams must also remediate and resolve the vulnerability. In some cases, remediation may only require a quick fix that can be manually applied without a major time commitment. In other cases, such as patch application, the fix may represent a major effort requiring a significant investment in time by DBAs to research, plan, test, and apply the fix. If a single vulnerability applies to a large population of databases, it may be necessary to apply the same fix or patch in a repetitive manner across many database instances, increasing the time investment even further.

The configuration management application allows organizations to create baseline configurations as standard, policy-based builds.

Standard builds improve control and stability and help maintain compliance. A Configuration Management Database (CMDB) manages the database configuration baselines by detailing critical build characteristics (such as configuration settings, patch levels, and user rights). Once a database standard build is certified, tested, and established, remediation requirements are minimized because the task is reduced to restoring the database to its original configuration baseline consistent with policy.

Through standard builds, configuration management helps the DBA team maintain databases in a state of continuous compliance. But challenges still exist. In larger organizations, where DBA tasks are carried out by separate teams who may operate independently or across multiple organizations, inconsistent outcomes may occur. Because we are human, fixes applied manually are inherently more prone to errors as tasks are performed by individuals with different levels of proficiency. To address this challenge, some configuration management solutions automate the fix process saving time and improving quality. Because it is based on business rules, permission sets, and scripted process, configuration management ensures consistency, uniformity, and eliminates human error.

Faced with ever-growing work backlogs, DBA teams recognize the opportunity not only to achieve dramatic productivity gains, but also to deliver more consistent outcomes with improved quality. As an essential element of database SRC, configuration management delivers extreme solution value and striking return on investment impact.

Data Masking

It is not surprising that nonproduction data is very often the target of a breach, and high profile thefts show that insiders do most of the damage.[lxvii]Sometimes the culprit is a disgruntled employee, but other times, sensitive test and development data containing personally identifiable information inadvertently ends up on a misplaced or stolen laptop, or is lost through outsourcing. With so much personally identifiable information from financial, healthcare, and government sources moving around in nonproduction environments, how can we ensure the privacy and security of sensitive data, and comply with government regulations and industry guidelines?

PCI DSS 6.3.4 dictates: "Production data cannot be used for testing or development." But if nonproduction database instances are most typically "clones" of production databases, how are we able to protect sensitive data in nonproduction environments? And how do we enable outsourced development teams and consultants to work on projects at home or on laptops without exposing the enterprise to unauthorized access of PII?

Many organizations have turned to data masking, a technique used to substitute confidential information with fictionalized data. Data masking removes personally identifiable information such as a person's name and account, credit card, or social security number, and transforms it into contextually accurate, albeit fictionalized, data. By obfuscating the information, data masking de-identifies personally identifiable information. Because it is no longer confidential, the masked data is now acceptable for use in nonproduction environments, such as development and testing.

Proper data masking routines propagate changes to nonproduction environments with consistently formatted, but fictionalized, data across all application environments. By de-identifying sensitive data in nonproduction environments, data masking effectively protects personally identifiable information, and satisfies regulatory guidelines (such as PCI DSS 6.3.4).

Database Encryption

Often considered a safe harbor for compliance requirements such as PCI DSS and HIPAA, database encryption has been broadly endorsed to lock down sensitive data. Tier-one database vendors generally offer database encryption as a built-in feature because many compliance guidelines require it.

While encryption may seem an obvious solution to secure data from loss, the management of encryption programs can become a complex burden (and may not even protect data in some cases).

Four areas of management focus must be considered before rolling out database encryption:

First, key management is a critical element of any encryption program. As data becomes encrypted, it must also be decrypted. With each additional encryption implementation, failsafe key management policies and procedures are required to ensure that backup, recovery, and normal application processing can be effectively maintained.

As more data is encrypted key management challenges grow, and the risk to data continuity increases. Improper or inconsistent key deployments may cause disruptions across multiple applications spanning the enterprise. Furthermore, as each database platform features native encryption, key management programs must become vendor/platform specific. Database SRC teams must operate with great discipline to ensure availability, and enterprise-wide key management processes must be robust.

The second critical management challenge of database encryption is application transparency. The consequences of encrypting a column of data are not trivial, and when database encryption is embedded into applications, unintended results are possible. At no time is it acceptable for database encryption to impact application performance. Support challenges accelerate when applications return an error, or when dependent programs crash suddenly because they fail to read encrypted data.

Application transparency means that the application need not be aware that it is dealing with encrypted data. As a result, no special handling or application maintenance is required. When processing against fields of data that are encrypted or inconsistent, some programs may not function as intended. For such applications encryption may not be an appropriate choice.

Policy management is a third area of focus. Effective encryption policy must be closely managed and aligned with the data lifecycle plan. In some cases separate protection policies for production, backup, and archive may need to be established. Such encryption policies must be carefully catalogued and maintained to avoid service disruptions, as once again, application continuity is a primary requirement.

Throughout its life cycle, data propagates across enterprise computing platforms. As functions such as backups and log files are created, decryption complexity must be carefully managed by policies. When encrypted data moves (for instance, to a sub-system running on another computing environment), decryption may be required, or the data may become unusable or lost. The data/key association must never be broken and policies must be carefully conceived to ensure that critical data does not become inadvertently encrypted forever!

The fourth area of focus is performance. Oftentimes encryption scopes are limited to a single column of personally identifiable data such as a social security number. But when scopes expand, and multiple encrypted columns of data are added to processing requirements, application performance may be impacted, sometimes unacceptably. In some cases protection policies may call for entire volumes to be encrypted, and job schedules may need to be adjusted as a result.

So, while database encryption is intuitively an important database SRC solution, there are also many dependencies. In certain use cases database encryption may be extremely effective, but in other more broadly defined cases it may be disqualified on account of excessive management overhead and complexity. Encryption policies must be application aware, and managed consistently to ensure data processing continuity.

Audit and Threat Management

Audit and threat management is primarily a forensic process to manage and track all activity in the database, and there are four separate strategies for deployment. Database activity monitoring (DAM), intrusion detection systems (IDS), and intrusion prevention systems (IPS) are agent-based technologies and support real time alerting of any database activity. Native audit is an agentless approach designed to leverage the existing audit and logging mechanisms built into the database management system (DBMS) itself.

Audit and threat management is further defined by six critical scopes:

- *Access and authentication auditing* determines who accessed which systems, when, and how.
- *Activity auditing* determines what activities were performed in the database by all users including administrators.
- *Threat auditing* monitors and provides forensic reporting on attempts to exploit known vulnerabilities in the database.
- *Change auditing* establishes a baseline policy for the database configuration, schema, users, privileges and structure, and then tracks any change or deviations from that baseline.

- *Complex attack and threat alerting* alerts when malicious activity is observed.

- *Misuse and malicious behavior prevention* prevents misuse and malicious activity.

Let's take a closer look at each strategy for audit and threat management.

Native Audit

Native audit is an agentless technology that collects database activity by writing to logs that trace database operations. Because it is agentless and does not require the installation of foreign software, native audit solutions are less intrusive, and implementations are less complex.

Performance, however, is a critical concern. As native audit mirrors every database activity by writing out to audit logs, significant overhead is placed on system resources, and severe performance impacts are possible. Database publishers have attempted to mitigate this performance concern by offering fine-grained controls to tune performance, but the undesirable impact of such an incremental processing load persists. While such tuning means improved results are possible, performance and scalability concerns still limit the acceptability of native audit for mission critical OLTP applications.

High performance and scalability, nonetheless, are not the only critical requirements. Effective audit solutions must also stand up to forensic examination, and they must feature strong separation of duty controls to prevent "the fox from watching the hen house." Some native audit solutions grant privileged users the authority to turn the system on and off. In such a scenario, malicious users with privileged authority are able to temporarily shut down native auditing and clear a path for malicious behavior. With no compensating control in place, such privileged users are able to commit malicious acts against the database undetected. Once the malicious activity is complete, the native audit system can be reengaged as if nothing ever happened.

The separation of duty violation exists because privileged users are able to defeat the very same control intended to monitor their behavior. The duties of the database administrator and the security administrator should be clearly divided, and authorities must be granted and attested to separately. To provide assurance that the activity of privileged database administrators will always be monitored through native auditing, only the security administrator should be able to disable native auditing.

But even when performance and segregation of duty controls are managed appropriately, native audit solutions still pose the problem of how to wade through the mountains of data collected in the log. Native audit solutions shipped with the database lack robust reporting, and data warehouse solution architectures may be required to scale the large volumes of data collected. Furthermore, enterprise wide reporting for database SRC requires support for heterogeneous database environments, and native audit solutions lack the cross-platform capability to produce a single version of the truth

Database Activity Monitoring (DAM)

When originally conceived less than ten years ago, DAM solutions were designed to compensate for the deficiencies of native auditing. Since their early incarnation, native audit environments have been vilified as system hogs that place unacceptable performance impact on OLTP environments, create mountains of difficult to read log data, and lack basic operational controls (such as separation of duty). DAM, on the other hand, tracks database activity without forcing the database to write each SQL statement out to a log. DAM also provides audit-ready reporting and features role-based security control. As a result DAM is able to monitor database activity with superior operational results.

But just because DAM is able to monitor all database activity does not mean an organization should do so (or would even want to!). Excessive database activity monitoring, whether it is based on native audit logs or DAM, can impact database and network performance and create output data overload on the backend. On the flip side, under-configured monitoring scopes may create audit gaps. The optimum configuration, therefore, should be based on the minimum scope required. As a result, monitoring rules, determined by separately administered policies, must provide filtering so SRC teams are able to manage scopes appropriately.

Host versus Network-Based DAM

Imagine the lock on the back door is broken and cannot be repaired until next Tuesday. By placing a camera on the door, at least some degree of compensating control can be maintained by monitoring who enters or leaves. The same forensic concept is used to establish a compensating control for privileged users. At some level, universal access to the database is absolutely necessary, so compensating control must be provided to monitor the activity of privileged users. Whether deployed as a host-based agent or a network-resident sensor, DAM is an essential capability, and database auditors maintain this area as a key focus.

Sometimes the remediation of database vulnerabilities is not immediately possible. Software patches may not be available, or a fix may simply not be possible. When separation of duty and least privilege access vulnerabilities are known to exist, DAM is the last line of defense.

Network-based DAM solutions are ideally suited for less demanding audit scopes. By parsing network SQL traffic and looking for malicious code strings and signatures of known attacks, network-based DAM is able to first identify and then alert or block malicious behavior. As a result, network-based DAM systems are often deployed for intrusion detection (IDS) or intrusion prevention (IPS). However, network-based DAM faces a critical limitation because it is only able to monitor SQL traffic on the network, and not inside the database itself. Such a scenario creates a major audit gap since database administrators still have the ability to log on to a database directly, and issue commands locally without ever traversing the network. Because it is unable to detect local host based SQL traffic, network-based DAM is not an adequate compensating control for privileged user monitoring.

Host-based DAM, on the other hand, tracks activity from within the database itself, and is therefore able to monitor all activity of privileged users. Host-based DAM deploys an agent (or "host sensor") inside the database to monitor all SQL traffic without limitation. With wide spread acceptance, host-based DAM represents the most complete and effective compensating control for privileged user monitoring.

Intrusion Detection Systems (IDS)

Unlike audit tools intended for forensic analysis, IDS identifies unauthorized or malicious activity in real-time by proactively alerting suspicious database traffic. IDS fires alerts of unauthorized access to sensitive data and exceptions to database policies. For example, unauthorized actions (such as a database query that returns thousands of credit card numbers, or repeated failed logins that fall outside of a given threshold) may be identified as deviating from normal operations. Rules may be established (such as thresholds for the volume of returned records or the number of failed logon attempts) and associated with protection policies.

Configuration of IDS may also be driven by the threat knowledgebase or user-defined threat signatures. Once an attack is detected, IDS is able to terminate the offending user session and prevent harm. Privilege abuse, data manipulation, and data leakage may be configured as rules to alert unauthorized or suspicious activity. As a result, IDS offers a flexible and reliable mechanism to identify threats to sensitive data.

Intrusion Prevention Systems (IPS)

Intrusion Prevention Systems (IPS) proactively prevent malicious behavior by blocking blacklisted activity. IPS provides real-time enforcement and preempts transactions that violate security policies.

A rules engine is at the core of the IPS system. Rules based on permission sets are configured within policies to initiate blocking of SQL commands. In addition IPS is able to trigger proactive measures such as automated lockouts of database users and VPN port shutdowns.

While IPS offers strong prevention capability, it may also be susceptible to false positives. Because user applications sessions are so inherently dynamic, blacklisting usage behaviors can be problematic and wreak havoc when legitimate users are prevented from valid activity. In addition, some IPS technologies that rely on "learning mode" to recognize malicious behavior may face critical deficiencies. For instance, what happens if an attack were to occur when the system was set to learning mode? Would the attack signature be white-listed from that time forward? Let's hope not! Despite the cliché that "an ounce of prevention is worth a pound of cure," such inherent limitations of IPS have contributed to tepid market acceptance of the technology and pushback from DBA teams.

Analytics

Ultimately, the solution value of database SRC is realized through effective reporting. Throughout the database SRC lifecycle, data is collected—lots of data—and the ability to correlate and synthesize such data into usable reports is what drives the solution value. Auditors seek a single version of the truth to establish levels of compliance. No matter the output format, database SRC reporting must establish the evidentiary foundation upon which security, risk, and compliance findings may be rendered.

Because the volumes of data to manage may be so large, database SRC requires robust data warehouse architecture to support not only standard reporting, but ad hoc and custom reporting as well. Database SRC systems must track and be accountable for every asset, password, user activity, entitlement, privilege, and configuration setting.

Many organizations, regardless of industry or regulatory affiliation, seek to establish custom policies for database SRC. Uniquely defined reports based on individual corporate policies must sometimes be produced. As a result, database SRC reporting must not only be flexible and adaptable, it must also be capable of extremely specific, user defined outputs.

With so many different regulatory requirements driving the reporting use case, highly specialized formats and notations are often required, and each compliance regulation carries its own specific requirements. Reporting formats must therefore map outputs to specific call outs for each regulation. For example, US Department of Defense personnel, auditors, and contractors often present DISA STIG (Defense Information Systems Agency—Security Technical Implementation Guide) reports to demonstrate compliance with DOD Directive 8500.1. By presenting reports with proper DISA STIG notations, DOD information assurance initiatives are more easily understood and able to demonstrate compliance.

Even though enterprises are subject to many different compliance regulations in many different formats, database SRC platforms must still deliver a single version of the truth for security, risk, and compliance. For example, just because an organization is not a DOD department does not mean that DISA STIG compliance is not a requirement. Contractors and suppliers to the DOD may find that DISA STIG compliance is a contract requirement. If that same DOD contractor is also a health care processor, and a public company managing credit card payments, they may also be obligated to comply with SOX, HIPAA, and PCI guidelines. To meet such diverse requirements database SRC platforms must support the widest possible range of compliance reporting outputs.

The Database SRC Application Platform

Before the innovation of enterprise resource planning (ERP) systems, best-of-breed approaches to enterprise accounting automated one functional application area at a time. Finance departments selected general ledger applications from one vendor and accounts receivables from another and succeeded in substantially reducing costs and improving the effectiveness of enterprise accounting. But the best-of-breed solution approach was also clumsy and inefficient. Periodic batch processing across dissimilar systems was required to produce complete financial statements and to meet reporting requirements. The end result was a new set of IT requirements to deliver costly, complex, and custom integrations between the point solutions.

To solve these challenges and deliver online processing for financial information, SAP and Oracle introduced ERP solutions that were architected so that all financial applications were integrated and shared a common database. Although certain batch processing routines were still required, the pieces nicely fit together. ERP succeeded in reducing the cost and improving the effectiveness of enterprise accounting even further. The rest of the story is history as the world seized on the benefits of a single version of the truth for enterprise financial information. Such integrated systems launched the age of ERP, and we have never looked back since.

Database SRC solutions have evolved similarly to ERP. Initial database SRC deployments focused on point solutions such as DAM, but as database SRC requirements evolved integrated functionality became necessary. Standalone database SRC applications may successfully meet point requirements, but are not sufficient to provide a complete solution by themselves. By integrating the different database SRC application modules together, the platform approach achieves a higher level of operational performance, reduces cost and ultimately ensures improved protection results.

When operated independently or standalone, database SRC applications lack context. For instance, standalone IDS solutions require integration with the threat knowledgebase in order to recognize threat profiles and attack signatures. Furthermore, by leveraging policies and vulnerability scans, IDS solutions can be tuned for optimal results. Despite the claims of self-learning IDS approaches, the only certain way to reduce IDS alarm false positives is through correlation with known threat signatures and exploits.

Just as financial applications reduced costs and improved efficiency through ERP, database SRC applications operate more efficiently and effectively when they share common, integrated database architecture. By leveraging the integration of one application against another, database SRC applications gain context and consistency, and achieve a single version of the truth.

Figure 19: The database SRC application platform.

Chapter 8

DATABASE SRC IN THE CLOUD

"Organizations that outsource their IT management and support also outsource a great deal of trust to these partners." [lxviii]

In their research document "The Cloud Wars: $100+ billion at Stake," Merrill Lynch predicts that by 2011 the cloud computing market will reach $160 billion in revenue.[lxix] Some say that the unprecedented hype surrounding this new paradigm stems from the disruptive departure cloud computing represents from traditional computing and operational processes. Cloud computing offers important on-demand benefits such as "pay-as-you-go" and self-service where capacity is elastic and applications are deployed without regard to underlying architecture.

The evolution of software to a service delivery model frees users from the limitations of traditional infrastructure such as scalability, performance bottlenecks, and capacity. But these are the business implications of the cloud paradigm. What are the underlying technology and operational implications? How do we enable database SRC in the cloud?

Whether cloud computing is delivered from a public, private, or hybrid cloud model, the underlying infrastructure is built upon the same technical building blocks as before. Behind the curtain of every cloud-computing model we still find software, servers, storage frames, and networks built and integrated by the same suppliers as before. Databases still require backups, software patches must still be applied, and "super users" must still be entitled with universal access to manage operations. What has changed?

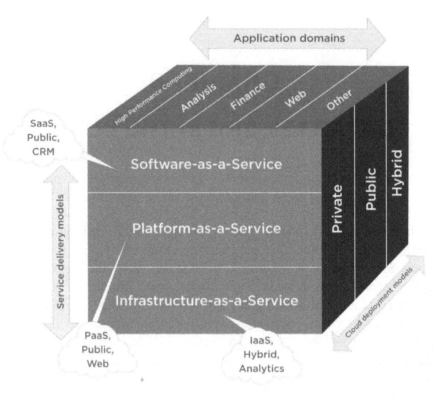

Figure 20: Cloud computing delivery frameworks. [lxx]

For one thing, cloud computing leverages virtualization, especially in regard to private cloud architectures. Originally conceived as a means to improve the resource utilization of expensive mainframe environments, virtual machine (VM) architectures deliver dramatic improvements in scalability and reduce operational cost. Virtualization simplifies server and systems management and enables computing grids which dramatically improve the utilization of computing resources. Through virtualization organizations are able to make more efficient use of infrastructure and to dramatically reduce physical footprints and power requirements.

Private cloud architectures utilize next generation data center designs and leverage virtualization to reduce the cost and complexity of running thousands of servers and thousands of database instances. "Hypervisors" are deployed to monitor and control operational complexity. Since computing is now managed as an elastic resource, the operational environment becomes highly dynamic. In virtualized environments servers may be provisioned and decommissioned with relative ease and at far less cost than traditional operating environments.

Data center automation and configuration management tools automate manual steps and reduce server and database build times from hours/days to minutes. Self-service models for system and database administration reduce IT costs even further. But such flexibility requires that control processes keep pace with such a dynamic and complex environment.

Multi-tenancy is another change introduced by the cloud. Many public cloud implementations feature multi-tenant database and application layers. Multi-tenancy enables end user subscribers to share common system resources such as databases and application programs. Because fewer application and database instances are maintained, systems management requirements are reduced, and operations are able to scale at lower cost and with less complexity. Similarly, multi-tenancy also reduces the cost and complexity of database SRC. Fewer database instances mean that database SRC teams deal with fewer vulnerabilities overall in the form of misconfigurations, patch gaps and excessive privilege grants. But database SRC best practices do not change in cloud computing. They just need to scale and adjust to a more dynamic environment.

Understanding the hype of cloud computing is not difficult when we recognize the organizational gain achieved by delegating certain non core tasks and authorities to a service provider. Public cloud models delegate infrastructure and systems management services to a vendor/service provider freeing the end-user organization to focus on the core activities that really drive their business. Why should a furniture manufacturer devote dedicated resources to running a CRM system when they may achieve improved results at a lower cost from a cloud service? The result is an on-demand model where operational effectiveness improves because software is delivered as a service.

Private clouds disrupt traditional cost models by improving the efficiency of internal operations and by delegating controls and processes to application owners. Data center automation and self-service delivery models enable application owners to take on an increasing share of the operational responsibility, thus reducing centralized IT cost.

Whether we delegate operational controls to application owners through self-service, or to vendor/service providers in public cloud models, we must always ensure proper governance for database SRC:

- Discovery, asset management, and inventory of sensitive data
- Classification of data and policy management
- Vulnerability assessment
- Access control and user entitlement management
- Configuration management
- Database activity monitoring of privileged users
- Audit and threat management
- Enterprise-wide reporting and analytics

Even though database SRC in the cloud shares fundamental operational requirements with traditional computing, database SRC in the cloud also represents business model change. Cloud computing enables the delegation of operational responsibility for the computing environment. But who is responsible for database SRC? Should self service subscribers be expected to manage the responsibility for database SRC on their own? Public cloud models suggest that the cost and complexity of database SRC is lowest when managed centrally in a multi-tenant environment.

Regardless of the cloud delivery model, the requirement to protect sensitive data remains. For the same reasons that subscribers come to the cloud in the first place, the complexity of compliance mandates is pushing increased levels of database SRC service authority to cloud providers. For example, The Federal Risk and Authorization Management Program (FedRAMP) is a key component of the Obama Administration cloud computing initiative. FedRAMP is driven by the US General Services Administration in association with the CIO Council and sets guidelines and security authorizations for US Government agencies to deploy cloud computing and monitor shared systems. Scheduled to be launched in the first quarter of 2011, FedRAMP fundamentally establishes the National Institute of Standards and Technology's Special Publication 800-53R (NIST 800-53) as the compliance framework for cloud computing in the US Federal Government. Under FedRAMP guidelines US Federal agencies are compelled to deploy database SRC controls for cloud computing in compliance with NIST 800-53 just as they are required to do in traditional computing environments. NIST 800-53 is a mandatory, non-waiverable compliance standard developed in response to the Federal Information Security Management Act (FISMA) of 2002.

Cloud applications are managed with special attention to service level agreements (SLA). SLAs are contract agreements that specify the commitments of the service provider relative to operating and delivering cloud computing at a predefined level of service. Failure to deliver at the predefined level of service generally results in fee credits paid back to the end user, but this can also include indemnifications and legal liabilities as well.

While SLA contracts may offer comfort and protection, the operational capability of a cloud-computing provider to deliver against SLAs must be carefully reviewed when selecting a vendor. Cloud users are urged to check references, and ensure that a robust defense-in-depth security model is in place. Such models should utilize tier-one software systems and proven processes based on best practices. Disaster recovery and data backup guarantees should be in place, and the vendor must maintain a comprehensive information assurance program with established database SRC controls. SAS 70 Type II audits should be current, be performed semiannually, and be accessible to cloud subscribers on demand. For US Government subscribers of cloud services, SLA coverage should also include substantiation of NIST 800-53 compliance as set forth by FedRAMP.

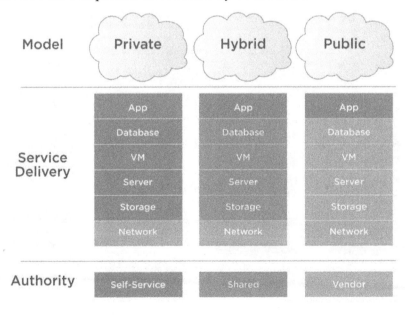

Figure 21:Governance authority and service delegation in the cloud.

At the end of the day, who is responsible for ensuring database security in the cloud? In private cloud environments certain database SRC operations may be delegated to application owners as self-service models transform traditional roles. In public or hybrid models, subscribers may rely more heavily on third party service providers to fill operational roles. Regardless of cloud models, multi-tenancy and virtualization, the ultimate responsibility for database SRC in the cloud rests as always with the owner of the sensitive data.

The responsibility to comply with PCI DSS, FedRAMP or SOX is not absolved because a database containing sensitive financial information or credit card information is deployed in the cloud. Control processes governing privileged users and the entitlement of user rights must still be maintained as audit authorities insist that organizations maintain an effective database SRC program whether databases are deployed in the cloud or not. In fact cloud computing offers opportunities for database SRC teams to achieve improved results at lower cost and to improve the delivery of proper controls. But the scope of responsibility and the delegation of authority to administer database SRC in the cloud must be established. SLA contracts must clearly specify roles and responsibilities and ensure proper accountability is in place.

DATABASE SRC IS CRITICAL FOR SECURING THE CLOUD

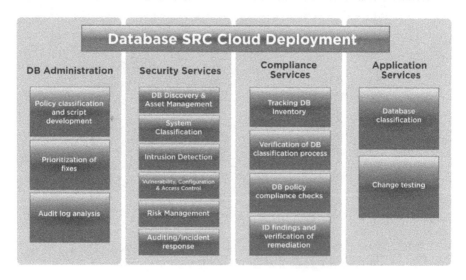

Figure 22: Roles and responsibilities for database SRC in the cloud.

Are databases in the cloud safer? Or are they less safe? How can we be certain that the cloud will successfully manage the ever-increasing threats and compliance challenges? DarkReading reports that in a recent survey of IT professionals by PhoneFactor, "73 percent said security was the primary obstacle to their adopting cloud computing, followed by compliance (54 percent) and portability and ownership of data (48 percent). Most say they were worried about stopping unauthorized access to their company data in the cloud, and 42 percent say security worries have stopped their organizations from going to the cloud."[lxxi]

Database SRC then has become a table stake capability and critical success factor for cloud computing. The high risk of data breach and compliance/audit failure requires that an effective database SRC program be operational in both cloud and traditional computing environments. The ultimate responsibility for database SRC in the cloud remains with the application owners, of course, because they own the data. But service delegation models, multi-tenancy and SLA contracts represent important opportunities to improve efficiency and service levels overall.

Chapter 9

DATABASE SRC SOLUTION VALUE

"Some projects will always feel like a trip to the dentist, but the good news is that having your teeth cleaned never paid off so well."

Prior to the adoption of a database SRC program, organizations must gain consensus and alignment between the business leadership and the rest of the IT team. Conflicting priorities are always a challenge, especially when budgets are tight, so a clear value proposition and a compelling business case must be developed to move the database SRC program forward. The scope, objectives, and approach of the project must be well defined, and the business case must be crystal clear. Even more importantly, success metrics such as performance levels and internal rate of return must be evident in order for the business case to be accepted and a successful transformation to occur.

Security, risk, and compliance projects have historically enjoyed relative immunity from the high level of prioritization and scrutiny received by many other IT initiatives. Often considered a "must have" requirement, database SRC initiatives have been viewed as a form of insurance similar to catastrophic health care. But as organizations gain a broader understanding into the range of solutions available, a sense of conflicting priorities can emerge. *Defense in depth* suggests layers of protection must be deployed at the network, operating system, and database level. Intuitively, data must be protected in the database where it lives, but compelling arguments exist for other priorities as well. So, why should organizations decide that database SRC is the number one priority versus many other compelling alternatives?

The defense in depth argument suggests that data must be protected when at rest, as well as when in motion. As a result essential requirements—including email filtering, network vulnerability, and data leak prevention (to name just a few)—emerge as competing priorities. Database SRC stands out as the priority because, in addition to protecting data where it lives, it delivers outstanding solution value in four key areas:

First, agentless database SRC applications deliver near immediate time-to-value. In contrast to solutions that require complex and extensive up front planning followed by protracted implementation efforts, database SRC scanning projects can be implemented in relatively short order, and are able to scale across thousands of database servers from the initial implementation. Because they are agentless applications, database asset management, policy management, vulnerability assessment, and user rights management can all be implemented quickly, and large networks of databases can be scanned in a single job. Database SRC controls are established as soon as the first scan is complete, and evidence of continuous compliance for SOX, HIPAA, GLBA, or PCI can be established.

Second, DBA and CISO teams are able to achieve productivity improvements and cost reduction synergies. Database SRC should not be categorized simply as an insurance policy against getting hacked (or even worse) as a necessary expense to keep auditors at bay. Like a trip to the dentist, database SRC is sometimes viewed as painful, but absolutely required to prevent much more horrible problems down the road. While the dentist analogy certainly fits, database SRC projects are generally not thought of as cost reduction initiatives. A closer look, however, reveals that database SRC projects are in fact quite capable of strong return on investment (ROI) and a compelling internal rate of return (IRR).

For example, DBA and CISO teams are already tasked with policy management, user rights management, and configuration management. Nevertheless, quite often these efforts are performed manually. Database SRC platforms that are able to automate many of the same tasks that DBA and CISO teams otherwise carry out manually may produce dramatic cost savings for organizations.

It is worthwhile to consider how much time DBA and CISO teams spend performing the following activities:

- Creating and cataloging security policies for databases
- Maintaining and updating scripts to uncover patches
- Researching and creating scripts to address configuration vulnerabilities

- Preparing reports for auditors, security, and compliance initiatives
- Determining access levels based on least privilege
- Discovering database instances that require a patch
- Managing passwords and permissions
- Researching patches and fixes to vulnerabilities
- Reconciling authorized changes to the database versus actual changes
- Provisioning, patching and configuring databases

Some projects will always feel like a trip to the dentist, but the good news is that having your teeth cleaned never paid off so well. Organizations can expect significant productivity gains and cost reductions by automating many of the mundane, day-to-day issues of database management. Typically, such savings and productivity gains are not as straightforward and easily calculated. Organizations emerge from database SRC projects more secure and in an audit-ready state of continuous compliance.

The third area of solution value is the reduction of audit cost and expense. In the absence of a database SRC platform to establish a continuous compliance process across the enterprise, IT auditors must perform specific audits on individual database instances. Such a one-off, point-and-shoot approach can not only take up to 120 man hours per database instance, but still the result is an incomplete picture that may leave 99 percent of the enterprise database scope unaudited. Audit scope can be approached either as a deep audit on individual database instances, or as an analysis into the integrity of the database SRC control process itself. Continuous compliance means the database SRC control process itself is the audit scope. Instead of "point-and-shoot" manual audits performed on each specific instance, database SRC platforms offer automated, online, evidentiary reports for all databases across the enterprise. As opposed to mining specific databases instances for configuration vulnerabilities and access controls, auditors run reports for PCI, SOX, HIPAA or other compliance frameworks on all the databases. Auditors can now reallocate time and effort—previously spent on individual database instances—to scale the audit scope dramatically across the enterprise.

Database SRC achieves the fourth area of solution value by extending an umbrella of protection across the entire enterprise. Again, a database is only as secure as its *weakest link,* and database SRC scopes must include every instance on the network as opposed to a few targeted instances. Too often, however, database SRC scopes are limited to a few high priority instances due to resource constraints. The effort required to manually lock down databases one instance at a time is just too great, and the cost of partial deployments can be tremendous when the source of the breach is found to be a non production or out-of-scope instance.

Database SRC solution value is greatest when platforms are designed to scale across the entire enterprise. By leveraging the database SRC platform against enterprise scopes, sensitive data is more secure and the productivity gains of DBA and CISO teams are pronounced. When managed as standard builds database configuration management workloads are reduced and these teams are freed up to perform higher level activities. While the ROI value of enterprise risk management may be difficult to establish, the hard cost savings of reduced audit expense are tangible and can be easily measured. For some organizations governance activities such as database SRC will continue to be managed as an insurance policy based on actuarial risk. But the ability to manage and deploy governance policies enterprise wide offers economy of scale, and database SRC projects offer a rich opportunity to reduce costs and improve operational results.

Chapter 10

SAVE THE DATABASE, SAVE THE WORLD!

"I just couldn't believe it happened to us, of all companies."
- Heartland Payment Systems CEO Bob Carr [lxxii]

There can be no question that the Internet has changed everything. Almost overnight, every person on earth has gained near unlimited access to the enormous computing power of the Internet. High-profile scandals like Enron and WorldCom have driven the need for Sarbanes-Oxley to ensure that public companies implement and maintain robust internal controls. And the harsh age of computer hackers has arrived. Albert Gonzalez has met justice, but who will be the next high profile cyber terrorist to create headlines? Will the next war be a cyber war? Some say it has already started.

Nonetheless, we seem to be living with a false sense of security, perhaps even in a state of denial. Eighty-four percent of organizations surveyed believe they have adequate security in place, yet 56 percent have been breached in the last twelve months, and 73 percent expect the attacks to increase. [lxxiii] Like the Maginot Line, which proved so strategically ineffective in preventing the German invasion of France in World War II, too many corporate security plans rely on "super secure" networks to protect sensitive data.

Despite billions and billions of dollars being spent thus far on IT security, over 428 million records were still breached [lxxiv] in the last two years alone at a cost to society of $204 each. [lxxv] And the evidence shows that the problem is accelerating. Clearly, we must admit that we have failed to secure our sensitive data. "Super secure" networks are most certainly necessary, and may even successfully defend against a direct attack, but they are not sufficient to defend against the "flanking attack" of a credentialed user. Once authorized on the network, credentialed attackers are able to proceed to the database relatively unobstructed and harvest sensitive data in droves.

As Verizon Business points out, 92% of records breached were lost from databases, so why aren't we doing more to secure sensitive data where it lives - in the database. Research published by Application Security, Inc. reveals that through 2010 fewer than 10 percent of the world's databases are properly secured with database SRC controls. Yes, "super secure" networks are a critical protection, but it makes no sense to lock the front door and leave the back door open. Network and perimeter defense strategies must evolve to prioritize sensitive data protection in the database.

The claxon has sounded, and watershed events such as the Heartland Payment Systems breach demand the broad adoption of enhanced corporate security, risk, and compliance programs. In an interview with BankInfoSecurity. com, Heartland CEO Bob Carr said, "I just couldn't believe it happened to us, of all companies."[lxxvi] Many executives responsible for data protection share Mr. Carr's false sense of security. His company operated as one of the 84 percent who felt their security was adequate, and then became one of the 54 percent who have been breached in the last year. For all those who feel they may have proper security in place, the Heartland Payment Systems breach serves as a brazen example of how extensive the damage can become. By the time it was over one hundred million credit cards were compromised and Heartland Payment Systems not only saw its brand and reputation damaged, they were forced to pay over one hundred million dollars in fines.

The job to save the database and save the world must be managed as a priority as opposed to a hedge game based in actuarial risk. But whose risk is it, anyway? Is it the risk to a DBA or security engineer to keep their job? Or is it the risk faced by corporations of possible fines and brand damage? For governments it may be the risk to national defense or the failure to perform their civic duty. Certainly the risk is quite broad, and willingly or not, must be shared by all.

Former NSA Director, Lt. General Ken Minihan suggests, "We should do all that we can to ensure trusted database security solutions are in place to protect our strategic coin." General Minihan says further that the "stakes are unacceptably high… and without a strategic defense doctrine, the threat of cyber war has become not only more likely, but much more dangerous." To counter the threat to national security, General Minihan has proposed a five point program in the foreword of *Save The Database, Save The World!*

1. *Re-establish our strategic defense doctrine to counter the emerging cyber threat.* How do we monitor and protect the public Internet while at the same time balance our essential democratic freedoms? When should a cyber attack be declared an act of war? When is a cyber attack the legitimate domain of law enforcement? What is the role of civilian business's versus the government? How do we manage the difficult attribution question when the identity of the attacker is often unclear, and how do we apportion the responsibilities to defend the various battle spaces?

2. *Evolve the scope of our cyber security initiatives to prioritize database protection.* For years network centric approaches have dominated our cyber security agenda, and today "super secure" networks form the vanguard of protection for our most critical infrastructure assets. Yet successful attacks and threat levels remain on the rise. Why? Because our adversaries are attacking the database, where our defenses are the weakest!

3. *Examine and create the authorities for conflict in the information age.* While it is clear that the Department of Homeland Security is responsible to defend our non-defense related government networks and databases, who is responsible for defending the critical infrastructure that operates in the private sector? And of equal importance, what are the authorities granted to the private sector to defend themselves? If an active defensive capability is not authorized for the private sector, then why not?

4. *Extend the NSA and Department of Defense umbrella of protection to include our entire critical infrastructure, including that which resides within the U. S. private sector.* Our nation cannot compromise when it comes to protecting our power grids, financial systems and critical industrial complex from a devastating online attack. The technical challenges of extending the DoD protection umbrella are

important, but not insurmountable. Political challenges, on the other hand, may prove more difficult. As we take action to achieve appropriate levels of defense, the American people must also be satisfied that their constitutional rights and freedoms will not be undermined in the process.

5. *Enhance and extend the authorities for the oversight and regulation of information systems where the general welfare of the public is at stake.* Many private enterprises and institutions properly lock down their sensitive data and IT infrastructure today simply because it is the right thing to do. Other businesses are proactive in defending themselves because they seek a competitive advantage. Unfortunately, the vast majority of businesses remain vulnerable because they are focused on other priorities, and this is unlikely to change until a proper system of incentives and enforceable mandates is put in place.

Which of the several bills currently before the US Congress should anchor our policy? Should government be able to shut down the public internet on Presidential "kill switch" authority, or would such a measure of protection over reach and infringe upon our essential democratic freedoms? Regardless of the ultimate outcome of the political debate, improved standards and authorities must be put in place before meaningful progress can be achieved.

Some say database security is a moral obligation because ordinary people deserve protection from losing their identity, their credit rating, or their most sensitive personal information such as their health care records. When ordinary people hand over their personal information to an institution that then loads it into a database, it just seems right that the institution should recognize the privacy rights of individuals and protect personal information without compromise.

Others say that database SRC carries legal implications that, so far, have not been thoroughly vetted or explored. Can we really isolate the cost of a breach to $204 per record? Or are there other liabilities as well, once we consider the indirect and consequential damages to individuals whose personal privacy has been breached or to corporations whose competitiveness has been compromised? How do we monetize the harm to individuals and corporations whose reputation has been damaged, or have been denied certain benefits, or who have been wronged because their personal or corporate information was compromised through a data breach? What type of liabilities or infringements could result through the misconduct or negligence of an organization whose job it was to protect personal information? Under what circumstances might a database administrator or security engineer face personal liability or charges of negligence when they fail to meet their obligation to protect sensitive information?

With the growth of social networking sites worldwide, the privacy rights of hundreds of millions of ordinary people are now in the spotlight. Caught in the crosshairs of questionable business practices by social network operators and state-sponsored attacks, users of these systems are left with little to no assurance that their valuable personal information is safe. In a very public way, Google, Facebook, and Twitter have become the front lines of Internet freedom, and users of those applications have learned that data privacy is necessary to protect individuals from business, society, and even their own governments.

As a response to high profile breaches of personal information at Google, Facebook, and other popular websites, consumers are rising up. The annual Computers, Freedom, and Privacy (CFP) conference created a Users' Bill of Rights[lxxvii] which includes the following mandates:

1. **Honesty:** Honor your privacy policy and terms of service.
2. **Clarity:** Make sure that policies, terms of service, and settings are easy to find and understand.
3. **Freedom of speech:** Do not delete or modify my data without a clear policy and justification.
4. **Empowerment:** Support assistive technologies and universal accessibility.
5. **Self-protection:** Support privacy-enhancing technologies.
6. **Data minimization:** Minimize the information I am required to provide and share with others.
7. **Control:** Let me control my data, and don't facilitate sharing it unless I agree first.

8. **Predictability:** Obtain my prior consent before significantly changing who can see my data.

9. **Data portability:** Make it easy for me to obtain a copy of my data.

10. **Protection:** Treat my data as securely as your own confidential data (unless I choose to share it), and notify me if it is compromised.

11. **Right to know:** Show me how you are using my data and allow me to see who and what has access to it.

12. **Right to self-define:** Let me create more than one identity and use pseudonyms. Do not link them without my permission.

13. **Right to appeal:** Allow me to appeal punitive actions.

14. **Right to withdraw:** Allow me to delete my account and remove my data.[lxxviii]

How corporations and government institutions will react remains to be seen, although calls for an Internet Bill of Rights, enhanced legal remedies, and a sense of moral obligation to protect sensitive data are growing. While the founding fathers who drafted the United States Bill of Rights never imagined that data privacy represented an inalienable right, surely they would have had they been on Facebook.

Thus far, the oversight of database SRC has been driven largely through industry self-regulation, and we must now acknowledge that such efforts have failed. Organizations such as the Payment Card Industry (PCI) Security Standards Council have established the Data Security Standard (DSS), but the results thus far are mixed at best. As the Ponemon study revealed, "Seventy-one percent of companies do not treat PCI as a strategic initiative, and 79 percent of those same companies have also experienced a data breach."[lxxix] Survey after survey reveals that despite compliance initiatives such as PCI, the problem is steadily and dramatically growing worse. Obviously the question must be asked whether industry is capable of regulating database security, risk, and compliance for itself, or if industry self-regulation is, in fact, the ultimate case of the "fox watching the henhouse."

In addition to concerns regarding oversight, questions also exist regarding enforcement. With little enforcement being driven through US Federal authorities, and bowing to pressure to protect the data privacy rights of ordinary citizens, several states have enacted their own legislation to govern the protection of personally identifiable information. On March 1, 2010, the State of Massachusetts enacted MASS 201 as a landmark data privacy law. However, months later, no prosecutions from the Massachusetts Attorney General's office have been concluded. The HITECH Act, voted into law by the US Congress as part of the American Recovery and Reinvestment Act of 2009, represented one of the first enforceable provisions regarding the protection of personal healthcare information (PHI). Yet, it was not until a year and a half later that the first fine was administered by Connecticut Attorney General Richard Blumenthal for a breach of 1.5 million records at Heath Net.

Over ten million databases across the globe remain largely unprotected. The scope of the problem is immense, and bold leadership is required to take effective action. Organizations must set priorities, train their teams, and launch protection projects. We must fight back against the bad guys and harden our database infrastructure to limit the points to attack. Just as no one would ever imagine operating a laptop today without an anti-virus scanner, every database must be locked down.

While the challenge to protect sensitive data is significant, viable solutions are available. The time has arrived to lay down a plan to protect our sensitive data in the database where it lives. Failure is just not an option! The protection programs we launch must be scalable and capable to protect large numbers of database servers across heterogeneous environments. These programs must be reliable, serviceable, and manageable. Furthermore, they must be affordable, and must offer the fastest time-to-value.

Nearly everyone has a role to play, but in many cases those roles lack clarity. Certainly the role of corporate management to step up and protect the sensitive data that is driving their business franchise is clear, but what happens when an attack is known to be state sponsored? Cloud computing models offer opportunities for improved protections, but service providers must step up to the challenge. When foreign government operatives hack into power grids, or private business such as Google, which government body carries the mandate to respond? The Department of Defense? The Department of Homeland Security? The United Nations? NATO?

The lack of clarity in US Government policy and its strategy to fight cyber war is striking. Again, Obama Administration Cyber Security Coordinator Howard Schmidt "isn't buying into the grim forecasts that the United States is ill-prepared to defend the government's and nation's critical information assets…" [lxxx]Yet on June 27, 2010, CIA Director Leon Panetta stated, "We are now in a world in which cyber warfare is very real. It could threaten our grid system… our financial system."[lxxxi] With no clear authorities in place today, corporations are left with no option except to mobilize, form cyber militias, and defend themselves.

And then there is the essential challenge of attribution. Who is behind three million unauthorized probes against the US Department of Defense networks every day? And who is attacking the power grids? Are these rogue criminal acts, or are they really acts of war conducted by state sponsored cyber warriors? Are we *already* engaged in a cyber war that is raging undeclared?

In an article he published in *The Washington Post,* Former Director of National Intelligence, Vice Admiral Michael McConnell recommends closer cooperation between the public and private sectors. To build a more effective cyber strategy capable to serve both military and private sector requirements, Vice Admiral McConnell recommends that leadership teams both in and outside of government work together to build a more practical and successful strategy framework.

"We now need a dialogue among business, civil society and government on the challenges we face in cyber space—spanning international law, privacy, and civil liberties, security, and the architecture of the Internet. The results should shape our cyber security strategy," McConnell writes. [lxxxii]

We all know what the hackers, evil doers, and cyber warriors are after. They want our data. They seek illegal profit, personal financial gain, military superiority, and competitive advantage. While we may never be truly safe from this threat, we can take effective action to protect our sensitive information. It is time to fight back and protect our data at its source—in the database.

Save The Database, Save The World!

SOURCES

[i]SDA Report. "A Conversation on Cybersecurity With William J. Lynn III, US Deputy Secretary of Defense"(September 15, 2010) http://www.securitydefenceagenda.org/Portals/7/2010/Events/Lynn/Lynn_Report.pdf

[ii] Lynn, William J. "Defending A New Domain." *Foreign Affairs* (September/October 2011) http://www.foreignaffairs.com/articles/66552/william-j-lynn-iii/defending-a-new-domain

[iii]Statement of General Keith B. Alexander Commander United States Cyber Command Before The House Committee On Armed Services. PDF (September 23, 2010) http://www.defense.gov/home/features/2010/0410_cybersec/docs/USCC%20Command%20Posture%20Statement_HASC_22SEP10_FINAL%20_OMB%20Approved_.pdf

[iv]Verizon Risk Team and the United States Secret Service "Verizon 2010 Data Breach Report: A study conducted by the Verizon Risk Team in cooperation with the United States Secret Service."(July 2010) http://www.verizonbusiness.com/resources/reports/rp_2010-data-breach-report_en_xg.pdf

Verizon Risk Team. "2009 Data Breach Investigations Supplemental Report: A Study Conducted by the Verizon Business RISK Team" (Janaury 2009) http://www.zdnetasia.com/whitepaper/2009-data-breach-investigations-supplemental-report-a-study-conducted-by-the-verizon-business-risk-team_wp-1388067.htm

[v] Ponemon Institute. "Fifth Annual US Cost of Data Breach Study – Benchmark Study of Companies." (January 2010) http://www.ponemon.org/data-security

[vi] Wright, Lawrence. "The Spymaster." *The New Yorker.*(January 21, 2008) http://www.newyorker.com/reporting/2008/01/21/080121fa_fact_wright

[vii]2011 Database Security Deployment Report. Application Security, Inc. (January 2011)

[viii] "Verizon 2009 and 2010 Data Breach Report"

[ix]2011 Database Security Deployment Report. Application Security, Inc. (January 2011

[x] Martínez-Cabrera, Alejandro. "How Some Ex-Employees Turn to Cybercrime." *San Francisco Chronicle.*(April 8, 2010) http://articles.sfgate.com/2010-04-08/business/20839989_1_breaches-data-enforcers

[xi] Verizon 2010 Data Breach Report. A study conducted by the Verizon Risk Team in cooperation with the United States Secret Service." July 2010

[xii] Verizon 2009 and 2010 Data Breach Report."

[xiii] Erdely, Sabrina. "Sex, Drugs, and the Biggest Cybercrime of All Time." *Rolling Stone.* (November 11, 2010). http://www.rollingstone.com/culture/news/sex-drugs-and-the-biggest-cybercrime-of-all-time-20101111

[xiv] Verini, James. "The Great Cyberheist." *The New York Times.*(Nov 10, 2010)

http://www.nytimes.com/2010/11/14/magazine/14Hacker-t.html?_r=1

[xv] Verini, James. "The Great Cyberheist." *The New York Times.*(November 10, 2010)

http://www.nytimes.com/2010/11/14/magazine/14Hacker-t.html?_r=1

[xvi] Verini, James. "The Great Cyberheist." *The New York Times.*(November 10, 2010)

http://www.nytimes.com/2010/11/14/magazine/14Hacker-t.html?_r=1

[xvii] Wikipedia. "Gonzalez, Albert." Wikipedia (August 2009)http://en.wikipedia.org/wiki/Albert_Gonzalez

[xviii] Wikipedia. *"Gonzalez, Albert."* Wikipedia. Wikipedia August 2009. Web. http://en.wikipedia.org/wiki/Albert_Gonzalez

[xix] Verizon 2010 Data Breach Report."

[xx] Krekel, Bryan. "Capability of the People's Republic of China to Conduct Cyber Warfare and Computer Network Exploitation." Northrop Grumman Corporation Report Prepared for the US-China Economic and Security Review Commission. (October 2009) http://www.uscc.gov/researchpapers/2009/NorthropGrumman_PRC_Cyber_Paper_FINAL_Approved%20Report_16Oct2009.pdf.

[xxi] Alexander, General Keith. "Cybersecurity Discussion with General Keith B. Alexander, Director of the NSA, Commander of US Cyber Command." *Center for Strategic and International Studies, Washington, DC.*(June 3, 2010) http://csis.org/event/cybersecurity-discussion-general-keith-b-alexander-director-national-security-agency

[xxii] Graham-Harrison, Emma and Buckley, Chris. "UPDATE 2-China PLA officer urges new Internet control agency."(Reuters)(February 22, 2010)http://www.reuters.com/article/idUSTOE61L04U20100222

[xxiii]Krekel, Bryan. "Capability of the People's Republic of China to Conduct Cyber Warfare and Computer Network Exploitation." *Northrop Grumman Corporation Report Prepared for the US-China Economic and Security Review Commission.*(October 2009) Pg. 31.

[xxiv] Krekel, Bryan. "Capability of the People's Republic of China to Conduct Cyber Warfare and Computer Network Exploitation." *Northrop Grumman Corporation Report Prepared for the US-China Economic and Security Review Commission.*(October 2009) Pg. 6.

[xxv]Heike, "Inside The World Of Chinese Hackers." *The Dark Visitor.* (August 17, 2009)
http://www.thedarkvisitor.com/page/4/

[xxvi] Krekel, Bryan. "Capability of the People's Republic of China to Conduct Cyber Warfare and Computer Network Exploitation." *Northrop Grumman Corporation Report Prepared for the US-China Economic and Security Review Commission.* (October 2009) p.23

[xxvii] Krekel, Bryan. "Capability of the People's Republic of China to Conduct Cyber Warfare." Pg. 67

[xxviii] Paller, Alan. "Utilities are Contested Territories." *Energy Biz.* March/April 2010.
http://www.nxtbook.com/nxtbooks/energycentral/energybiz0310/index.php?startid=47#/48

[xxix] Paller, Alan. "Utilities are Contested Territories."

[xxx] Chabrow, Eric. "Howard Schmidt Dismisses Cyber War Fears". *GovInfoSecurity.com* March 6, 2010.
http://www.govinfosecurity.com/articles.php?art_id=2267

[xxxi] Chabrow, Eric. "Howard Schmidt Dismisses Cyber War Fears".

[xxxii]Oltsik, John. "Database Security and Compliance Risks." ESG Market Research. December 2009

[xxxiii] Oltsik, John. "Database Security and Compliance Risks." *ESG Market Research.* December 2009

[xxxiv] Yuhanna, Noel. "Your Enterprise Database Security Strategy 2010." *Forrester Research.* Boston, MA. (2010)

[xxxv]Wikipedia. Maginot Line: http://en.wikipedia.org/wiki/Maginot_Line

[xxxvi] Pescatore, John. "High-Profile Thefts Show Insiders Do the Most Damage." *Gartner Group.* (November 2002)

[xxxvii] Verizon Business Risk Team. "2009 Data Breach Investigations Report." (January 2009)

xxxviii Ponemon Institute. "2008-2009 Fourth Annual US Cost of Data Breach Study – Benchmark Study of Companies."(January 2009)

xxxix Ponemon Institute. "Fifth Annual US Cost of Data Breach Study – Benchmark Study of Companies." (January 2010)

xl Kurtz, Paul. "Cyber Security Industry Alliance Survey Results." Business Week. (October 2006)

http://www.businessweek.com/technology/content/oct2006/tc20061017_457028.htm

xli Ponemon Institute. "2009 PCI DSS Compliance Survey." September 2009.

xlii Ponemon Institute. "2009 PCI DSS Compliance Survey." September 2009.

xliii"Verizon 2010 Data Breach Report."

xliv"Virus-Like Attack Hits Web Traffic." *BBC Technology Online World Edition.* (January 2003)
http://news.bbc.co.uk/2/hi/technology/2693925.stm

xlv Boutin, Paul. "Slammed!" *Wired.* (July 2003)http://www.wired.com/wired/archive/11.07/slammer.html

xlvi Boutin, Paul. "Slammed!"

xlvii Moscaritolo, Angela. "Octomom's Hospital Fined." *SCMagazine.* (May 2009) http://www.scmagazineus.com/octomoms-hospital-fined/article/136934/

xlviiiChickowski, Ericka. "Thwarting SQL Injection Threats: New Dark Reading report explores what database developers and database administrators can do about the pervasive SQL injection attack."*DarkReading.(*November 2, 2009) http://www.darkreading.com/story/showArticle.jhtml?articleID=221400279

xlix Chickowski, Ericka "Thwarting SQL Injection Threats". DarkReading..

l Verizon 2010 Data Breach Report."

li Carr, Jim. "Mass SQL Injection Attack Compromises 70,000 Websites". *SCMagazine.* (January 2008) http://www.scmagazineus.com/mass-sql-injection-attack-compromises-70000-websites/article/100497/

lii Chickowski, Ericka. "SQL Injection: A Major Threat to Data Security." *DarkReading.* (April 2010)http://www.darkreading.com/database-security/167901020/security/application-security/221400279/index.html

liii Shaul, Josh. Application Security Inc. Presentation

liv Chickowski, Ericka. "SQL Injection: A Major Threat to Data Security"

lv Barnett, Ryan Breach Security. "The State of Web Security Issues". *ComputerWorld.* (February 2010)

[lvi] Harper, Mitchell. "SQL Injection Attacks – Are You Safe?" *Sitepoint.* June 2002.

[lvii] Poulson, Kevin and Zetter, Kim. "U.S. Intelligence Analyst Arrested in Wikileaks Video Probe." *Wired Magazine* (June 6, 2010)

http://www.wired.com/threatlevel/2010/06/leak/

[lviii] Johnson, M. Eric. "Information Risk in the Professional Services." Pg. 2

[lix] Johnson, M. Eric. "Information Risk in the Professional Services." Pg. 2

[lx] Johnson, M. Eric. "Information Risk in the Professional Services." Pg. 2

[lxi] Poulsen, Kevin and Zetter, Kim. "U.S. Intelligence Analyst Arrested in Wikileaks Video Probe". *Wired Magazine* (June 6, 2010)

http://www.wired.com/threatlevel/2010/06/leak/

[lxii] Sandhu, Ravi and David Ferraiolo, and Richard Kuhn."The NIST Model for Role-Based Access Conrol: Toward a United Standard.". *NIST* http://csrc.nist.gov/staff/Kuhn/towards-std.pdf

[lxiii]Wilson, Clark. "Clark Wilson Integrity Model."*Stanford* http://theory.stanford.edu/~ninghui/courses/Fall03/papers/clark_wilson.pdf

[lxiv]"Verizon 2010 Data Breach Report."

[lxv]"Verizon 2010 Data Breach Report."

[lxvi]"Verizon 2010 Data Breach Report."

[lxvii] Pescatore, John. "High-Profile Thefts Show Insiders Do the Most Damage". *Gartner Group.* (November 2002)

[lxviii]"Verizon 2010 Data Breach Report."

[lxix] Merrill Lynch Research Team. "The Cloud Wars: $100+ billion At Stake.*"Merrill Lynch Research Note.* (May 2008)

[lxx] Mather, Tim, Kumaraswamy, Subra and Katif, Shahed. "Cloud Security and Privacy: An Enterprise Perspective on Risks and Compliance." (California: O'Reilly Media, 2009)

[lxxi]Jackson, Kelly. "Cloud Security Market To Reach $1.5 Billion In Next Five Years."

Dark Reading (October 21, 2010http://www.darkreading.com/security-services/167801101/security/application-security/227900512/index.html

[lxxii] Field, Tom. "CEO Discusses Lessons Learned from Historic Data Breach" *BankInfoSecurity.com.* (July 2010) http://www.bankinfosecurity.com/articles.php?art_id=2767

[lxxiii] Oltsik, John. "Database Security and Compliance Risks." *ESG Market Research*(December 2009)

[lxxiv]Verizon Risk Team and the United States Secret Service "Verizon 2010 Data Breach Report: A study conducted by the Verizon Risk Team in cooperation with the United States Secret Service."(July 2010) http://www.verizonbusiness.com/resources/reports/rp_2010-data-breach-report_en_xg.pdf

Verizon Risk Team. "2009 Data Breach Investigations Supplemental Report: A Study Conducted by the Verizon Business RISK Team" (Janaury 2009) http://www.zdnetasia.com/whitepaper/2009-data-breach-investigations-supplemental-report-a-study-conducted-by-the-verizon-business-risk-team_wp-1388067.htm

[lxxv]Ponemon Institute. "2008-2009 Fourth Annual U.S. Cost of Data Breach Study – Benchmark Study of Companies."(January 2009)

[lxxvi] Field, Tom. "CEO Discusses Lessons Learned from Historic Data Breach"

[lxxvii]Pincus, John. "Computers, Freedom, and Privacy - Social Network Users' Bill of Rights"

http://cfp.org/wordpress/?p=341

[lxxviii]Diana, Allison. "Social Networking Bill Of Rights Released" InformationWeek

(June 23, 2010)

http://www.informationweek.com/news/security/privacy/showArticle.jhtml?articleID=225701171

[lxxix] Ponemon Institute. "Fifth Annual US Cost of Data Breach Study – Benchmark Study of Companies."(January 2010)

[lxxx] Chabrow, Eric. "Howard Schmidt Dismisses Cyber War Fears". *GovInfoSecurity.com* March 6, 2010.http://www.govinfosecurity.com/articles.php?art_id=2267

[lxxxi] Tapper, Jake. "CIA: Cyber Warfare Could 'Paralyze' US" Interview with Leon Panetta"*ABC News*. (June 27, 2010)http://blogs.abcnews.com/politicalpunch/2010/06/cia-cyber-warfare-could-paralyze-us.html

[lxxxii] McConnell, Mike. "Mike McConnell on how to win the cyber-war we're losing". *Washington Post*. (February 28, 2010) http://www.washingtonpost.com/wp-dyn/content/article/2010/02/25/AR2010022502493.html

GLOSSARY

Advanced Information Warfare

SDSW Def – Used to establish control of an adversary's information flow and maintain battle space dominance in the midst of cyber warfare.

Advanced Persistent Threat

Wikipedia - In the computer security community, it is used to specifically refer to a sub-set of such threats, in a long-term pattern of targeted sophisticated hacking attacks aimed at governments, companies and political activists, and by extension, also to refer to the groups behind these attacks. A common misconception associated with the APT relates to its specificity to the targeting of Western governments. While examples of technological APT's against Western governments may be more publicized, this is incorrect, and the technological ('cyber') APT has been used by actors in many nations as a means to gather intelligence on individuals, and groups of individuals of interest.

Agentless deployment

SDSW Def – The deployment of foreign software, such as monitoring technology, either on the network or the host is typically referred to as an agent. An agent gathers information or performs some other service without the immediate presence of an operator. Agents search all or some part of a network, gather information, and present results based on preset parameters. Agentless applications require no foreign software to be deployed, and also carry the benefits of reduced system maintenance, improved overall system performance, and comprehensive security.

Asset Management

SDSW Def - The asset management application provides a complete inventory of all databases on the corporate network. Leveraging agentless, network-based scanning technology, asset management discovers and identifies every database using a standard pen test approach. Results are returned with fingerprints that are referenced against a knowledgebase to discover key identification characteristics such as the specific database publisher, release detail, and the business unit owner. Based on these results, an asset inventory is created.

Audit and Threat Management

SDSW Def – Comprised of four separate protection strategies to audit and log database management system (DBMS) activity:Database activity monitoring (DAM), intrusion detection systems (IDS), and intrusion prevention systems (IPS, all agent based), and Native Audit (agentless).

Authorized privileged user accounts

SDSW Def – Authorized privileged user accounts are created through a process of attestation and include database administrators, system administrators, database owners, consultants, contractors, and offshore developers. These accounts need to be identified, normal activity needs to be tracked, and these accounts need to be monitored for suspicious or unauthorized activity.

Authorized user accounts with excessive privileges

SDSW Def – Authorized user accounts with excessive privileges include users who have transferred to other positions in the organization, but still retain the privileged rights granted from the previous job, and users who have been granted excessive privileges by role inheritance, by accident, or by default. These accounts need to be clearly identified, and the rights adjusted as necessary.

Authentication

SearchSecurity/WhatIs.com - Authentication is the process of determining whether someone or something is, in fact, who or what it is declared to be. In private and public computer networks (including the Internet), authentication is commonly done through the use of logon passwords. Knowledge of the password is assumed to guarantee that the user is authentic.

Basel II

SearchSecurityUK/WhatIs.com - Basel II is an international business standard that requires financial institutions to maintain enough cash reserves to cover risks incurred by operations. The Basel accords are a series of recommendations on banking laws and regulations issued by the Basel Committee on Banking Supervision (BSBS). The name for the accords is derived from Basel, Switzerland, where the committee that maintains the accords meets.

Backdoor

SDSW Def - A method of gaining remote control of a victim's computer by reconfiguring legitimately installed software, or the installation of a specialized program designed to allow access under attacker-defined conditions. Trojan horse programs and rootkits often contain backdoor components.

Black Hat

SearchSecurityUK/WhatIs.com - Black hat is used to describe a hacker (or, if you prefer, cracker) who breaks into a computer system or network with malicious intent. Unlike a white hat hacker, the black hat hacker takes advantage of the break-in, perhaps destroying files or stealing data for some future purpose. The black hat hacker may also make the exploit known to other hackers and/or the public without notifying the victim. This gives others the opportunity to exploit the vulnerability before the organization is able to secure it.

Botnet

SearchSecurityUK/WhatIs.com - A botnet, otherwise known as a zombie army, a number of Internet computers that, although their owners are unaware of it, have been set up to forward transmissions (including spam or viruses) to other computers on the Internet. Any such computer is referred to as a zombie - in effect, a computer "robot" or "bot" that serves the wishes of some master spam or virus originator. Most computers compromised in this way are homebased.

Brute Force

SDSW Def – Tools that try to guess weak passwords by attempting logon combinations over and over until valid access is found.

Buffer Overflow

Wikipedia - A buffer overflow, or buffer overrun, is an anomaly where a program, while writing data to a buffer, overruns the buffer's boundary and overwrites adjacent memory. This may result in erratic program behavior, including memory access errors, incorrect results, program termination (a crash), or a breach of system security. Buffer overflows can be triggered by inputs that are designed to execute code, or alter the way the program operates. They are thus the basis of many software vulnerabilities and can be maliciously exploited. Bounds checking can prevent buffer overflows.

California Senate Bill 1386

California Senate Bill SB1386, amending civil codes 1798.29, 1798.82 and 1798.84 is a California law regulating the privacy of personal information. The law was introduced by California State Senator Peace on February 12, 2002, and became operative July 1, 2003. Essentially, the bill requires an agency, person, or business that conducts business in California and owns or licenses computerized "personal information" to disclose any breach of security (to any resident whose unencrypted data is believed to have been disclosed). The bill mandates various mechanisms and procedures with respect to many aspects of this scenario, subject also to other defined provisions.

Clickjacking

SDSW Def - Clickjacking (also known as *user-interface* or *UI redressing* and *IFRAME overlay*) is an exploit in which malicious coding is hidden beneath apparently legitimate buttons or other clickable content on a Website.

Cloud Computing

SDSW Def – Cloud computing offers important on-demand computing benefits including pay-as-you-go and self-service where capacity is elastic and applications are deployed without regard to underlying architecture. The evolution of software to a service delivery model frees users from the limitations of traditional infrastructure such as scalability, performance bottlenecks and capacity.

Common Criteria (CC)

NIST.gov - Common Criteria (CC) is an international set of guidelines and specifications developed for evaluating information security products, specifically to ensure they meet an agreed-upon security standard for government deployments. Common Criteria is more formally called "Common Criteria for Information Technology Security Evaluation."Common Criteria has two key components: Protection Profiles and Evaluation Assurance Levels. A Protection Profile (PPro) defines a standard set of security requirements for a specific type of product, such as a firewall. The Evaluation Assurance Level(EAL) defines how thoroughly the product is tested.

Compliance

SearchDataManagementUK/WhatIs.com - Compliance is either a state of being in accordance with established guidelines, specifications, or legislation or the process of becoming so. Software, for example, may be developed in compliance with specifications created by some standards body. In the legal system, compliance usually refers to behavior in accordance with legislation, such as the United States Can Spam Act of 2003, the Sarbanes-Oxley Act (SOX) of 2002, or HIPAA (United States Health Insurance Portability and Accountability Act of 1996). Compliance in a regulatory context is a prevalent business concern, perhaps because of an ever-increasing number of regulations and a fairly widespread lack of understanding about what is required for a company to be in compliance with new legislation.

Configuration Management

SDSW Def – The database configuration management application enables organizations to baseline configurations into standard builds based on policy. Standard builds improve control and stability and help maintain compliance. A Configuration Management Database (CMDB) manages the database configuration baselines by detailing critical build characteristics such as settings, patch levels and entitlements. Once the database standard build is certified, tested and established, remediation requirements are minimized because the task is reduced to restoring the database to its original configuration baseline set by policy.

Continuous Compliance

SDSW Def – Continuous compliance implies an inherently disciplined, proactive system based on best practices where documented controls, policy driven processes, reporting, and ongoing improvements are a standard operating procedure. In such an environment, organizations have established a framework of proactive measures which offers the best possible means of prevention.

Control Objectives for Information and Related Technology (COBIT)

Gartner - An auditing standard developed by the Information Security Audit and Control Association for assessing information security risk.

Corporate Governance

SearchCompliance/WhatIs.com - Corporate governance is a term that refers broadly to the rules, processes, or laws by which businesses are operated, regulated, and controlled. The term can refer to internal factors defined by the officers, stockholders or constitution of a corporation, as well as to external forces such as consumer groups, clients, and government regulations.

COSO

COSO.org - COSO is recognized the world over for providing guidance on critical aspects of organizational governance, business ethics, internal control, enterprise risk management, fraud, and financial reporting.

Cracker

SearchSoftwareQuality/WhatIs.com - A cracker is someone who breaks into someone else's computer system, often on a network;

bypasses passwords or licenses in computer programs; or in other ways intentionally breaches computer security. A cracker can be doing this for profit, maliciously, for some altruistic purpose or cause, or because the challenge is there. Some breaking-and-entering has been done ostensibly to point out weaknesses in a site's security system.

Critical Infrastructure Protection (CIP)

SDSW Def – The Critical Infrastructure Protection (CIP) program is designed to assure the security of critical infrastructures in the United States, and protect systems, networks and key assets from external attacks.

Cross-site Scripting (XSS)

SearchSoftwareQuality/WhatIs.com - Cross-site scripting, also known as XSS, is a security exploit in which the attacker inserts malicious coding into a link that appears to be from a trustworthy source. When someone clicks on the link, the embedded programming is submitted as part of the client's Web request and can execute on the user's computer, typically allowing the attacker to steal information.

Cyber criminals

SDSW Def – Criminals who use phishing attacks or any number of fraudulent means for acquiring passwords and usernames to gain credentialed network access. With network access achieved, hackers target the database where sensitive data lives and can be remotely harvested.

Cyber Security

SDSW Def – Cyber security is an arms race where each new advance by attackers is met by better defenses.

Cyber Security Coordinator

SDSW Def – US Government White House appointment with direct access to the President, looking at vulnerabilities and preventive measures to protect US businesses and consumers.

Cyber Security Industry Alliance (CSIA)

SDSW Def – Former watchdog and advocacy organization that merged with the AeA, ITAA, and GEA to form TechAmerica. Representing approximately 1,200 member companies of all sizes from the public and commercial sectors of the economy, TechAmerica is the industry's largest advocacy organization and is dedicated to helping members' top and bottom lines in the technology industry.

Cyber Warfare

SearchSecurity/WhatIs.com – Cyber warfare is Internet-based conflict involving politically motivated attacks on information and information systems. Cyber warfare attacks can disable official Websites and networks, disrupt or disable essential services, steal or alter classified data, and cripple financial systems -- among many other possibilities.

Data Masking

SDSW Def – Technique to substitute confidential information with fictionalized data. Data masking removes or transforms personally identifiable information such as name, account, credit card, or social security number into contextually accurate, but fictionalized, data. By obfuscating the information, data masking de-identifies personally identifiable information. Because it is no longer confidential, the masked data is now acceptable for use in nonproduction environments such as development and test.

Data Protection Act of 1998 (DPA) United Kingdom

Wikipedia - The Data Protection Act 1998 (DPA) is a United Kingdom Act of Parliament which defines UK law on the processing of data on identifiable living people. It is the centerpiece of legislation that governs the protection of personal data in the UK. Although the Act itself does not mention privacy, it was enacted to bring UK law into line with the European Directive of 1995 which required Member States to protect people's fundamental rights and freedoms and in particular their right to privacy with respect to the processing of personal data. In practice it provides a way for individuals to control information about themselves.

Database Administrators (DBA's)

SDSW Def – Database Administrators manage a variety of tasks related to adding/removing users from databases but also include reviewing data logs in search of anomalous activity; user rights review; scripting to manage configuration vulnerabilities and patch gaps; and information assurance to certify that databases conform to established SRC policy. Also testing application availability for users after configuration changes made to remediate vulnerabilities. Database Administrators are often thought of as privileged users who possess universal access to the database which requires compensating control.

Database Activity Monitoring (DAM)

SDSW Def – The Process of tracking network or host based SQL traffic without forcing the database to write out to logs. DAM also provides audit ready reporting and features role based security control. As a result DAM is able to monitor the necessary database activity with superior operational results.

Database SRC in the Cloud

SDSW Def – The process of deploying, patching and configuring database security, risk and compliance technology in a cloud-enabled or virtualized database environment.

Database SRC Life Cycle

SDSW Def –The database SRC life cycle is a best practices based program which involves an iterative process of discovery, policy management, vulnerability assessment, user rights review, prioritization of fixes, remediation, monitoring of known vulnerabilities and finally, deep reporting and analytics of the entire life cycle. The goal is to establish a process of continuous compliance.

Database SRC Solution Value

SDSW Def – The return on investment or internal rate of return, comprised of financial savings, protection of business assets, and strategic resource allocation that enterprise organizations receive through successful deployment and integration of a comprehensive database security risk and compliance platform.

Data Leakage Prevention (DLP)

CL - Network security market segment of network and/or endpoint policy-based technology where data is tagged as sensitive and then monitored for unauthorized access or usage. Remediation at points of egress or as part of the switching fabric is a common function of DLP solutions.

DB2 (IBM)

Ibm.com – Long considered to be the first database product to use SQL language, the IBM DB2 Enterprise Server Edition is a relational model database server developed by IBM. It primarily runs on Unix (namely AIX), Linux, system I (formerly known as/400), z/OS and Windows servers. DB2 also powers the different IBM InfoSphere Warehouse editions.

Defense in Depth

SearchSecurity/WhatIs.com - Defense in depth is the coordinated use of multiple security countermeasures to protect the integrity of the information assets in an enterprise. The strategy is based on the military principle that it is more difficult for an enemy to defeat a complex and multi-layered defense system than to penetrate a single barrier. Defense in depth minimizes the probability that the efforts of malicious hackers will succeed. Defense in Depth strategy helps system administrators and security personnel identify "true users" who attempt to compromise a computer, server, proprietary network or ISP (Internet service provider).

Denial of Service (DoS)

SDSW Def - A denial-of-service attack (DoS attack) or distributed denial-of-service attack (DDoS attack) is an attempt to make a computer resource unavailable to its intended users. Although the means to carry out, motives for, and targets of a DoS attack may vary, it generally consists of the concerted efforts of a person or people to prevent an Internet site or service from functioning efficiently or at all, temporarily or indefinitely.

DISA – Defense Information Systems Agency

www.disa.mil – The Defense Information Systems Agency, a Combat Support Agency, provides engineering, command and control, and enterprise infrastructure to continuously operate and assure a global net-centric enterprise in direct support to joint warfighters, National level leaders, and other mission and coalition partners across the full spectrum of operations.

DISA-STIG - Defense Information Systems Agency Security Technical Information Guides

www.disa.mil - DISA (the Defense Information Systems Agency) publishes a large number of STIGs (Security Technical Information Guides) that are designed to serve as the configuration standards for DOD (Department of Defense) IA (Intelligence Agency) and IA-enabled devices/systems.

Distributed Denial of Service (DDoS)

SDSW Def - A class of attacks that results in the exhaustion of computing or communications resources by engaging many intermediate computers to simultaneously attack one victim. These intermediate attack systems are often previously compromised and under the control of the attacker.

Enterprise Solution Architecture

SDSW Def – Architecture designed to manage cross-platform mission critical applications on multiple operating systems and databases from different suppliers. Also helps with managing compliance for databases running on heterogeneous environments, since SRC teams must manage separate and distinct policies which may be assigned to each database instance as a separate database.

Encryption

Gartner - The process of systematically encoding a bit stream before transmission so that an unauthorized party cannot decipher it.

Ethernet

Gartner - High-speed serial bus specification from the Institute of Electrical and Electronics Engineers.

EU Data Protection Directive

Wikipedia - The Data Protection Directive (officially Directive 95/46/EC on the protection of individuals with regard to the processing of personal data and on the free movement of such data) is a European Union directive which regulates the processing of personal data within the European Union. It is an important component of EU privacy and human rights law. The directive was implemented in 1995 by the European Commission. The responsibility for compliance rests on the shoulders of the "controller", meaning the natural or artificial person, public authority, agency or any other body which alone or jointly with others determines the purposes and means of the processing of personal data; (art. 2 d)

The data protection rules are applicable not only when the controller is established within the EU, but whenever the controller uses equipment situated within the EU in order to process data. (art. 4) Controllers from outside the EU, processing data in the EU, will have to follow data protection regulation. In principle, any online business trading with EU citizens would process some personal data and would be using equipment in the EU to process the data (i.e. the customer's computer).

Federal Risk and Authorization Management Program (FedRAMP)

CIO.gov - The Federal Risk and Authorization Management Program or FedRAMP has been established to provide a standard approach to Assessing and Authorizing (A&A) cloud computing services and products. FedRAMP allows joint authorizations and continuous security monitoring services for Government and Commercial cloud computing systems intended for multi-agency use. Joint authorization of cloud providers results in a common security risk model that can be leveraged across the Federal Government. The use of this common security risk model provides a consistent baseline for Cloud based technologies.

FERC -Federal Energy Regulatory Commission

Gartner - An independent agency aligned to the US Department of Energy that regulates the transmission and sale of energy utilities, such as oil and electricity.

FISMA – Federal Information Security Management Act

Nist.org - FISMA, the Federal Information Security Management Act, known also as requires each federal agency to develop, document, and implement an agency-wide program to provide information security for the information and information systems that support the operations and assets of the agency, including those provided or managed by another agency, contractor, or other source.

Also known as the E-Government Act (Public Law 107-347) passed by the 107th Congress and signed into law by the President in December 2002, FISMA was created to recognize the importance of information security to the economic and national security interests of the United States.

GLBA/FMA99 – Graham Leach Bliley Act/Financial Services Modernization Act of 1999

Gartner, Wikipedia - The Gramm-Leach Bliley Act, also known as FMA99 was signed into US law in November 1999, this legislation — also known as the "Gramm-Leach-Bliley Act," after the senators who sponsored it — allowed many financial institutions to engage in a broader spectrum of activities, but also placed additional restrictions on many of their practices, notably those related to privacy. The act established an "affirmative and continuing obligation" for FSPs to respect their customers' privacy, and to protect the confidentiality of their information — an aspect of the legislation that had a major impact on FSPs' customer information management practices and strategies.

"GUEST", "OPEN", and "PUBLIC" access

SDSW Def – On any network or operating system, there are varying levels of access as allowed by corporate IT policy, but also based on business need. Guest access is temporary access given to a non-regular employee on a certain network. Open access refers to access controls that remain open for anyone within a particular network. Public access refers to open access to the public, for example, a university system, or even a municipal library system.

Threat Knowledge Base

SDSW Def – Database SRC threat research is collected to form a knowledge base which is the central reference and repository for vulnerability checks, monitoring rules and fixes. A key differentiator of any database SRC environment, the threat knowledgebase is only as valuable and effective as the strength of the research behind the discovery, definition, testing and remediation of specific threats.

HIPAA (Health Insurance Portability and Accountability Act)

Gartner, SearchDataManagement – HIPAA, the Health Information Portability and Accountability Act was passed by the US congress in August 1996. HIPAA's directives call for the use of electronic data interchange (EDI) in healthcare transactions, and for protecting the privacy of patient healthcare information. There are two sections to the Act. HIPAA Title I deals with protecting health insurance coverage for people who lose or change jobs. HIPAA Title II includes an administrative simplification section which deals with the standardization of healthcare-related information systems. In the information technology industries, this section is what most people mean when they refer to HIPAA. HIPAA establishes mandatory regulations that require extensive changes to the way that health providers conduct business.

Host versus Network Based Database Activity Monitoring (DAM)

SDSW Def – Database Activity Monitoring (DAM) is the process by which software can be installed on either the host or network level to monitor activity in database applications. Host-based activity monitoring consists of monitoring sensors being installed at the host level so that monitoring activity is done through what is termed passive procedures, like inspecting configuration settings, password files and policy settings. Network-based activity monitoring detects malicious activity such as denial of service attacks, port scans or even attempts to crack into computers by monitoring network traffic.

Gonzalez, Albert

Wikipedia - Born in 1981, Albert Gonzalez is a computer hacker and computer criminal who is accused of masterminding the combined credit card theft and subsequent reselling of more than 170 million card and ATM numbers from 2005 through 2007—the biggest such fraud in history. Gonzalez and his accomplices used SQL injection techniques to create malware backdoors on several corporate systems in order to launch packet sniffing (specifically, ARP Spoofing) attacks which allowed him to steal computer data from internal corporate networks.

Hacker

SearchSecurity/WhatIs.com – The term hacker is used in popular media to describe someone who attempts to break into computer systems. Typically, this kind of hacker would be a proficient programmer or engineer with sufficient technical knowledge to understand the weak points in a security system.

The Health Information Technology for Economic and Clinical Health Act (HITECH) Act of 2009 (HITECH Act)

HIPAA Survival Guide, KPMG - Developed as part of the American Recovery and Reinvestment Act of 2009, the HITECH Act (Health Information Technology for Economic and Clinical Health) contains incentives related to health care information technology in general (e.g. creation of a national health care infrastructure) and contains specific incentives for healthcare providers and hospitals designed to accelerate the adoption of electronic health record (EHR) systems among providers. Because this legislation anticipates a massive expansion in the exchange of electronic protected health information (ePHI), the HITECH Act also widens the scope of privacy and security protections available under HIPAA; it increases the potential legal liability for non-compliance; and it provides for more enforcement.

Identity and Access Management (IAM)

Gartner - An identity management access (IAM) system is a framework for business processes that facilitates the management of electronic identities. The framework includes the technology needed to support identity management. IAM technology can be used to initiate, capture, record and manage user identities and their related access permissions in an automated fashion. This ensures that access privileges are granted according to one interpretation of policy and all individuals and services are properly authenticated, authorized and audited.

Infection kit

SearchSecurity/WhatIs.com – An infection kit is commonly referred to as a set of tools used to launch malware programs to corrupt files, alter or delete data, distribute confidential data, disable hardware, deny legitimate user access, and cause a hard drive to crash.

Infrastructure As A Service (IaaS)

SearchCloudComputing - Infrastructure as a Service (IaaS) is a provision model in which an organization outsources the equipment used to support operations, including storage, hardware, servers and networking components. The service provider owns the equipment and is responsible for housing, running and maintaining it. The client typically pays on a per-use basis. IAAS is one of three core components of cloud computing services deployment, which also includes Software as a Service (SaaS) and Platform as a Service (PaaS).

IDS (intrusion detection system)

SDSW Def – Unlike audit tools that are intended for forensic analysis, IDS identifies unauthorized or malicious activity in real time by proactively monitoring database traffic and alerting on suspicious activity. IDS alerts against such behavior as unauthorized access to sensitive data or security exceptions to database policies. For example, unauthorized actions such as a database query that returns thousands of credit card numbers, or repeated failed logins that fall outside of a given threshold can be identified as deviating from normal operations. Thresholds for the volume of returned records or the number of failed logon attempts can be established as alert rules and assigned to protection policies. Configuration of IDS can be driven either by the known threats in the SRC knowledgebase or by user defined threat signatures. Rules are created to alert on unauthorized and suspicious activity such as abuse of privilege, privilege escalation, data manipulation or leakage. As a result, IDS offers a flexible and reliable mechanism to identify and flag any suspicious, unusual or abnormal access to sensitive data and critical systems

Intrusion Prevention Systems (IPS)

Gartner – An Intrusion Prevention Systems (IPS) proactively prevents malicious behavior from occurring by blocking blacklisted or undesired activity. IPS provides real-time enforcement and preempts transactions that violate security policies. This is accomplished by configuring rules within policies which initiate blocking via permission sets of SQL commands and users. Automated lock-outs of database users and VPN port shutdowns are examples of IPS proactive measures and are configurable based on triggers and alerts.

Internal Auditors

Gartner - Databases are now included in the audit scope. Analysis and attestation of database entitlements; access control based on least privilege; privileged user activity auditing; separation of duty analysis; compliance with regulatory requirements; patch and configuration management practices according to established process and/or policy are all now compulsory at the database layer.

Integrated Application Platform

SDSW Def – To solve the challenges of effective enterprise accounting of and deliver online processing for financial information, SAP and Oracle introduced integrated ERP solutions which were architected so that all financial applications shared a common database. Although certain batch processing routines were still required, the pieces nicely fit together. The rest is history. The world quickly seized on the benefits of a single version of the truth for enterprise financial information. Through the integration of financial applications in to a single database instance, the age of enterprise resource planning (ERP) began, and we have never looked back. It is the goal of database SRC to operate as an integrated application platform.

ISO 27001

SearchDataCenter/WhatIs.com - ISO 27001 (formally known as *ISO/IEC 27001:2005*) is a specification for an information security management system (ISMS). An ISMS is a framework of policies and procedures that includes all legal, physical and technical controls involved in an organization's information risk management processes. According to its documentation, ISO 27001 was developed to "provide a model for establishing, implementing, operating, monitoring, reviewing, maintaining and improving an information security management system."

IT Executives

Gartner - Top management is responsible to prioritize security, risk and compliance initiatives; assess the overall vulnerability posture against compulsory compliance regulations (especially for public companies); ensure the protection of critical corporate database assets; protect brand and shareholder interests through information assurance (IA) initiatives.

Native Audit

SDSW Def – Native audit is an agentless technology which collects database activity by writing logs to trace normal database operations. Because it is agentless and operates as a standard database feature without the requirement to install foreign software, the native audit solution is non-intrusive and implementations are less complex. Performance is the primary shortcoming of native audit as system resources can be severely impacted if audit scope control parameters are not managed carefully.

NERC (North American Electric Reliability Corporation)

Nerc.com - The North American Electric Reliability Corporation's (NERC) mission is to ensure the reliability of the North American bulk power system. NERC is the electric reliability organization (ERO) certified by the Federal Energy Regulatory Commission to establish and enforce reliability standards for the bulk-power system. NERC develops and enforces reliability standards; assesses adequacy annually via a 10-year forecast, and summer and winter forecasts; monitors the bulk power system; and educates, trains and certifies industry personnel. ERO activities in Canada related to the reliability of the bulk-power system are recognized and overseen by the appropriate governmental authorities in that country.

NIST (National Institute of Standards and Technology)

NIST.org – NIST, the National Institute of Standards and Technology, established in 1901, is an agency of the US Department of Commerce as the nation's first federal physical science research laboratory. It was previously formed as the National Bureau of Standards.

NIST Special Publication 800.53 (NIST 800.53)

NIST.org -NIST Special Publication 800-53 (NIST 800.53) is a standard that sets security controls for information systems applications that involve the United States federal government. It is published by the National Institute of Standards and Technology, which is a non-regulatory agency of the United States Department of Commerce. Security controls are the management, operational, and technical safeguards or countermeasures prescribed for an information system to protect the confidentiality, integrity, and availability of the system and its information.

Litchfield Zero-Day

SDSW Def – David Litchfield is a well-known security researcher based in the UK who demonstrated an unpatched Oracle database vulnerability at the Black Hat/DEFCON 2010 conference in February 2010. Litchfield demonstrated a working exploit, thus making it publicly available for anyone to use against Oracle database 10g and newer. The vulnerable functionality within the product allowed anyone with a login to execute the exploit, otherwise phrased as executable by PUBLIC. At the time of the announcement, the vulnerability was unpatched by Oracle, but the company has since patched it through their Critical Patch Update (CPU) process.

Massachusetts 201 CMR 17 Data Protection Law

KPMG – A set of data protection and data breach notification standards established by the Commonwealth of Massachusetts that requires any business entity with Massachusetts residents' Personally Identifiable Information (PII) to comply with for paper and electronic records. The law went into effect on March 1, 2010.

Microsoft SQL Server

Microsoft.com - Microsoft SQL Server is Microsoft's relational model database server product. It offers a complete approach to managing, accessing and delivering information across the organization.

Multi-Factor Authentication

SDSW Def - Authentication is generally required to access secure data or enter a secure area. The requestor for access or entry shall authenticate himself based on proving authentically his identity by means of a PIN, password ID, or biometric data, such as a fingerprint. Multi-factor authentication refers to at least two or more authentication methods to increase the assurance that the bearer has been authorized to access secure systems.

MySQL

SearchEnterpriseLinux - MySQL is a relational database management system (RDBMS) based on SQL (Structured Query Language). First released in January, 1998, MySQL is now one component of parent company MySQL AB's product line of open source database servers and development tools.

National Intelligence

Dictionary of Military Terms, Department of Defense - Integrated departmental intelligence that covers the broad aspects of national policy and national security, is of concern to more than one department or agency, and transcends the exclusive competence of a single department or agency.

NATO (North Atlantic Treaty Organization)

Princeton University – NATO, the North Atlantic Treaty Organization is an international organization created in 1949 by the North Atlantic Treaty for purposes of collective security.

National Information Standards and Technology (NIST)

NIST.gov – The National Information Standards and Technology (NIST) is a unit of the US Department of Commerce. NIST promotes and maintains measurement standards. It also has active programs for encouraging and assisting industry and science to develop and use these standards.

National Vulnerability Database (NVD)

Wikipedia - The National Vulnerability Database is the US government repository of standards based vulnerability management data represented using the Security Content Automation Protocol (SCAP). This data enables automation of vulnerability management, security measurement, and compliance. NVD includes databases of security checklists, security related software flaws, misconfigurations, product names, and impact metrics. NVD supports the Information Security Automation Program (ISAP).

NIST Special Publication 800.53

NIST.gov - Special Publications in the 800 series as published by NIST (National Information Standards and Technology) present documents of general interest to the computer security community. The Special Publication 800 series was established in 1990 to provide a separate identity for information technology security publications. This Special Publication 800 series reports on ITL's research, guidelines, and outreach efforts in computer security, and its collaborative activities with industry, government, and academic organizations. Special Publication 800.53 is specifically targeted at Federal information systems...

OPAC (Open Public Access Catalog)

An OPAC (Online Public Access Catalog) is an online bibliography of a library collection that is available to the public. OPACs developed as stand-alone online catalogs, often from VT100 terminals to a mainframe library catalog. With the arrival of the Internet, most libraries have made their OPAC accessible from a server to users all over the world. User searches of an OPAC make use of the Z39.50 protocol. This protocol can also be used to link disparate OPCS into a single "union" OPAC.

Oracle Database

Oracle.com, Wikipedia – Oracle database is Oracle Corporation's enterprise database product line. The Oracle database system, identified by an alphanumeric system identifier or SID comprises at least one instance of the application, along with data storage. An instance, identified persistently by an instantiation number (or activation id: SYS.V_$DATABASE.ACTIVATION#), comprises a set of operating-system processes and memory-structures that interact with the storage. Typical processes include PMON (the process monitor) and SMON (the system monitor).

Password Attack, Password Cracking

SearchSecurity - Password attacks, otherwise known as password cracking, is the process of recovering passwords from data that has been stored in or transmitted by a computer system. A common approach is to repeatedly try guesses for the password. The purpose of password cracking might be to help a user recover a forgotten password (though installing an entirely new password is less of a security risk, but involves system administration privileges), to gain unauthorized access to a system, or as a preventive measure by system administrators to check for easily crackable passwords.

Payment Card Industry (PCI)

PCI Security Standards Council - PCI DSS, a set of comprehensive requirements for enhancing payment account data security, was developed by the founding payment brands of the PCI Security Standards Council, including American Express, Discover Financial Services, JCB International, MasterCard Worldwide and Visa Inc., to help facilitate the broad adoption of consistent data security measures on a global basis. The PCI DSS is a multifaceted security standard that includes requirements for security management, policies, procedures, network architecture, software design and other critical protective measures. This comprehensive standard is intended to help organizations proactively protect customer account data.

Personally Identifiable Information (PII)

SearchFinancialData/WhatIs.com - Personally identifiable information (PII) is any data about an individual that could, potentially identify that person, such as a name, fingerprints or other biometric data, email address, street address, telephone number or social security number.

Phishing

SearchSecurity/WhatIs.com - Phishing is an e-mail fraud method in which the perpetrator sends out legitimate-looking email in an attempt to gather personal and financial information from recipients. Typically, the messages appear to come from well-known and trustworthy Web sites. A phishing expedition, like the fishing expedition it's named for, is a speculative venture: the phisher puts the lure hoping to fool at least a few of the prey that encounter the bait, using different methods of social engineering and e-mail spoofing ploys to try to trick their victims into providing their personal and financial information, only to steal it.

Platform As A Service (PaaS)

SeachCloudComputing/WhatIs.com - Platform as a Service (PaaS) is a way to rent hardware, operating systems, storage and network capacity over the Internet. The service delivery model allows the customer to rent virtualized servers and associated services for running existing applications or developing and testing new ones.

Policy Management

SDSW Def – Using baselines from the database asset inventory and sensitive data discovery to establish a policy management framework. Database SRC policies are established by a centralized template to configure the rules and control parameters of protection. Templates may follow standard definitions to support common compliance regulations such as SOX and HIPAA, or organizations may edit or build custom database SRC policies based on internal standards. Once established the policy management system forms the backbone of a risk management framework for continuous compliance.

Privilege Escalation

SDSW Def – Where user database rights privileges are escalated outside of any control process either by circumventing database tracking tools, or more innocently through unintended role inheritance. Privilege escalation attacks are included in the same category of attacks as SQL injection attacks.

Risk Management

Forrester, Wikipedia - The process of determining the maximum acceptable level of overall risk to and from a proposed activity, then using risk assessment techniques to determine the initial level of risk and, if this is excessive, developing a strategy to ameliorate appropriate individual risks until the overall level of risk is reduced to an acceptable level.

Role Based Access Control (RBAC)

SearchSecurity - Role-based access control (RBAC) is a method of regulating access to computer or network resources based on the roles of individual users within an enterprise. In this context, access is the ability of an individual user to perform a specific task, such as view, create, or modify a file. Roles are defined according to job competency, authority, and responsibility within the enterprise.

Rootkit

SearchSecurity/WhatIs.com - A rootkit is a collection of tools (programs) that enable administrator-level access to a computer or computer network. Typically, a cracker installs a rootkit on a computer after first obtaining user-level access, either by exploiting a known vulnerability or cracking a password. Once the rootkit is installed, it allows the attacker to mask intrusion and gain root or privileged access to the computer and, possibly, other machines on the network. A rootkit may consist of spyware and other programs that: monitor traffic and keystrokes; create a "backdoor" into the system for the hacker's use; alter log files; attack other machines on the network; and alter existing system tools to escape detection.

SANS Institute

SANS.org - SANS is the most trusted and by far the largest source for information security training and certification in the world. It also develops, maintains, and makes available at no cost, the largest collection of research documents about various aspects of information security, and it operates the Internet's early warning system - Internet Storm Center.

Sarbanes-Oxley (SOX)

SearchCIO, SOX Forum.com - The Sarbanes-Oxley Act of 2002 (often shortened to *SOX*) is legislation enacted in response to the high-profile Enron and WorldCom financial scandals to protect shareholders and the general public from accounting errors and fraudulent practices in the enterprise. The act is administered by the Securities and Exchange Commission (SEC), which sets deadlines for compliance and publishes rules on requirements. Sarbanes-Oxley is not a set of business practices and does not specify how a business should store records; rather, it defines which records are to be stored and for how long.

Security Content Application Protocol (SCAP)

SearchSecurity/WhatIs.com - The Security Content Automation Protocol, also known as SCAP (pronounced es-kap) is a method for using specific standards to enable automated vulnerability management, measurement, and policy compliance evaluation (e.g., FISMA compliance). The National Vulnerability Database (NVD) is the US government content repository for SCAP.

Security Operations

Gartner - CISO teams must now assure that a full life cycle approach to database SRC is in place including the discovery and inventory database assets; performance of initial entitlement reviews; separation of duty and least privilege analysis; establishment of database SRC policies; identification, assessment and mitigation of security vulnerabilities; safeguarding of the enterprise against breaches by both authorized and unauthorized users.

Security Readiness Review(SRR)

Published and updated regularly by DISA (Defense Information Systems Agency), Security Readiness Review Scripts (SRRs) test products for STIG compliance. SRR (Security Readiness Review) Scripts are available for all operating systems and databases that have STIGs, and Web servers using IIS. The SRR scripts are unlicensed tools developed by the Field Security Office (FSO) and the use of these tools on products is completely at the user's own risk.

Security, Risk and Compliance (SRC)

SDSW Def – Security, Risk and Compliance (SRC) is the market category that corresponds to AppSec's approach to securing database assets while grounding database security in regulatory initiaitves. SRC is typically included in the full industry term 'Database SRC,' which stands for Database Security, Risk and Compliance, that signifies the comprehensive market category that AppSec started and maintains a leadership position in.

Sensitive Data Discovery

SDSW Def – The discovery process of locating and categorizing sensitive data. As a critical component of the asset management application, sensitive data discovery also serves other database SRC application domains including data masking, encryption, data leak prevention (DLP), policy management, user entitlement management, and vulnerability assessment. All these database SRC applications share a common requirement to understand information about sensitive data. Manual discovery is simply not feasible, and therefore the automated discovery must be intelligent. Not only must sensitive data be accurately documented, the discovery process must be smart enough to prevent false positive identifications. Exception values and discrepancies must be manageable, and rules engine processing is required so that the discovery process is able to derive values and become application aware.

Social engineering

Social engineering describes a non-technical kind of intrusion that relies heavily on human interaction and often involves tricking other people to break normal security procedures. A social engineer runs what used to be called a "con game." For example, a person using social engineering to break into a computer network would try to gain the confidence of someone who is authorized to access the network in order to get them to reveal information that compromises the network's security. They might call the authorized employee with some kind of urgent problem; social engineers often rely on the natural helpfulness of people as well as on their weaknesses. Additionally, social engineering relies on people's inability to keep up with a culture that relies heavily on information technology. Social engineers rely on the fact that people are not aware of the value of the information they possess and are careless about protecting it.

Software-as-a-Service (SaaS) as it differs from Managed Service and CPE

SearchCloudAsAService/WhatIs.com - Software as a Service (SaaS) is a software distribution model in which applications are hosted by a vendor or service provider and made available to customers over a network, typically the Internet. SaaS is becoming an increasingly prevalent delivery model as underlying technologies that support Web services and service-oriented architecture (SOA) mature and new developmental approaches, such as Ajax, become popular.

Spear Phishing

SearchSecurity/WhatIs.com - Spear phishing is an e-mail spoofing fraud attempt that targets a specific organization, seeking unauthorized access to confidential data. As with the e-mail messages used in regular phishing expeditions, spear phishing messages appear to come from a trusted source. Phishing messages usually appear to come from a large and well-known company or Web site with a broad membership base, like a large e-commerce site.

Spyware

Spyware is any technology that aids in gathering information about a person or organization without their knowledge. On the Internet (where it is sometimes called a *spybot* or *tracking software*), spyware is programming that is put in someone's computer to secretly gather information about the user and relay it to advertisers or other interested parties. Spyware can get in a computer as a software virus or as the result of installing a new program.

SQL Slammer Worm

Wikipedia - SQL Slammer is a computer worm that caused a denial of service on some Internet hosts and dramatically slowed down general Internet traffic, starting at 05:30 UTC on January 25, 2003. It spread rapidly, infecting most of its 75,000 victims within ten minutes. So named by Christopher J. Rouland, the CTO of ISS, Slammer was first brought to the attention of the public by Michael Bacarella. Although titled "SQL slammer worm", the program did not use the SQL language; it exploited a buffer overflow bug in Microsoft's flagship SQL Server and Desktop Engine database products, for which a patch had been released six months earlier.

Systems Network Architecture (SNA)

SearchDataCenter/WhatIs.com - Systems Network Architecture (SNA) is a proprietary IBM architecture and set of implementing products for network computing within an enterprise. It existed prior to and became part of IBM's Systems Application Architecture (SAA) and it is currently part of IBM's Open Blueprint. With the advent of multi-enterprise network computing, the Internet, and the de facto open network architecture of TCP/IP, IBM is finding ways to combine its own SNA within the enterprise with TCP/IP for applications in the larger network.

SQL (Structured Query Language)

SQL (Structured Query Language) is a standard interactive and programming language for getting information from and updating a database. Although SQL is both an ANSI and an ISO standard, many database products support SQL with proprietary extensions to the standard language. Queries take the form of a command language that lets you select, insert, update, find out the location of data, and so forth.

SQL Injection

Wikipedia, ThreatPost - SQL injection is a code injection technique that exploits a security vulnerability occurring in the database layer of an application. The vulnerability is present when user input is either incorrectly filtered for string literal escape characters embedded in SQL statements or user input is not strongly typed and thereby unexpectedly executed. It is an instance of a more general class of vulnerabilities that can occur whenever one programming or scripting language is embedded inside another. SQL injection attacks are also known as 'SQL insertion attacks.'

Sybase ASE

Sybase.com - Sybase Adaptive Server Enterprise (ASE) database Adaptive Server Enterprise (ASE) is a high-performance relational database management system for mission-critical, data-intensive environments. It ensures highest operational efficiency and throughput on a broad range of platforms. ASE key features include patented encryption, partitioning technology, patent-pending query technology for "smarter" transactions and continuous availability in clustered environments.

Unauthorized accounts with excessive privileges

SDSW Def – Often in any commercial or enterprise-class database environment, there are users with excessive privileges, meaning that they may have the capabilities to perform tasks that are unnecessary within the organization for them to perform their jobs. Additionally, there are often databases that are classified as unauthorized based on the information stored within those applications. When the toxic combination of excessive privileges coincides with unauthorized accounts in the database, the results could be catastrophic in terms of data loss if there are malicious insiders exploiting that data.

User Rights Management

SDSW Def – Through user rights management, separation of duty, compliance and the theory of least privilege can be managed and controlled for databases across the enterprise. Today, when audit teams examine separation of duty as it applies to databases, the role of privileged users is generally a central focus. DBA's assigned privileged user accounts represent a classic separation of duty audit finding. Since the least privilege for a database administrator to perform their job equates to universal privileges across the database, there is no way to resolve the vulnerability. Rights management offers a comprehensive solution by providing reports on the privileges of each user as well as details into who has what type of access to sensitive data. Armed with this information, SRC teams are able to identify all assigned privileges which are excessive, including those that are inherited, and revoke them if necessary. Such an assessment process allows the SRC team to maintain user entitlement rights as they were originally conceived during the initial entitlement review and flag changes for attestation.

US Department of Homeland Security (DHS)

DHS.gov - The United States Department of Homeland Security (DHS) is a Cabinet department of the United States Federal Government with the primary responsibilities of protecting the territory of the US from terrorist attacks and responding to natural disasters.

US Director of National Intelligence

Wikipedia - The Director of National Intelligence (DNI), is the United States government official subject to the authority, direction and control of the President, who is responsible under the Intelligence Reform and Terrorism Prevention Act of 2004 for:

- Serving as the principal adviser to the President, the National Security Council, and the Homeland Security Council for intelligence matters related to national security;
- Serving as the head of the sixteen-member Intelligence Community; and
- Overseeing and directing the National Intelligence Program.

US-China Economic and Security Review Commission (USCC)

www.uscc.gov - The US-China Economic and Security Review Commission (USCC) was established on October 30, 2000 by the Floyd D. Spence National Defense Authorization Act for 2001 specifically to monitor, investigate, and submit to congress an annual report on the national security implications of the bilateral trade and economic relationship between the United States and the People's Republic of China, and to provide recommendations, where appropriate, to Congress for legislative and administrative action.

Virtualization

SearchServerVirtualization/WhatIs.com - Virtualization is the creation of a virtual (rather than actual) version of something, such as an operating system, a server, a storage device or network resources. Operating system virtualization is the use of software to allow a piece of hardware to run multiple operating system images at the same time. The technology got its start on mainframes decades ago, allowing administrators to avoid wasting expensive processing power. Virtualization can be viewed as part of an overall trend in enterprise IT that includes autonomic computing, a scenario in which the IT environment will be able to manage itself based on perceived activity, and utility computing, in which computer processing power is seen as a utility that clients can pay for only as needed. The usual goal of virtualization is to centralize administrative tasks while improving scalability and workloads.

Vulnerability Assessment

SDSW Def – The vulnerability assessment application examines, reports, and proposes fixes for database security holes such as buffer overflows, password attacks, privilege escalations, unauthorized operating system access, and attack signatures and misconfiguration scenarios that constitute database threats. Identified issues include default or weak passwords, missing patches, poor access controls, and a host of other conditions. Through vulnerability assessment, a security, risk and compliance profile is established for each database in the enterprise. The vulnerability assessment application performs an agentless scan of the database settings, entitlements, passwords and configurations. By leveraging database SRC policies, checks are run against a threat knowledgebase which contains the research information required to reliably identify vulnerabilities, threats and audit exposures. The output from the scan is a list of vulnerabilities and threats prioritized by severity along with fix information. Organizations are delivered a current and reliable vulnerability profile against specific regulatory and audit requirements. Custom vulnerabilities or special tuning scans based on checks and rules for specific applications are also possible enabling enforcement of internal configuration standards.

Vulnerability Management

SearchSecurity/WhatIs.com - Vulnerability management is the cyclical practice of identifying, classifying, remediating, and mitigating vulnerabilities. This practice generally refers to software vulnerabilities in computing systems.

Web Application Firewalls (WAF)

Forrester, SearchSecurity - Web Application Firewalls (WAF's) are application-level firewalls implemented to control input, output, and/or access from, to, or by an application or service. It operates by monitoring and potentially blocking the input, output, or system service calls which do not meet the configured policy of the firewall. The application firewall is typically built to monitor one or more specific applications or services (such as a Web or database service), unlike a network firewall which can provide some access controls for nearly any kind of network traffic.

Wikileaks

Wikipedia - WikiLeaks is an international news media non-profit organisation that publishes submissions of private, secret, and classified media from anonymous news sources and news leaks. Its website, launched in 2006 and run by The Sunshine Press claimed a database of more than 1.2 million documents within a year of its launch. The organisation describes its founders as a mix of Chinese dissidents, journalists, mathematicians, and start-up company technologists from the United States, Taiwan, Europe, Australia, and South Africa. Julian Assange, an Australian Internet activist, is generally described as its director. WikiLeaks was originally launched as a user-editable wiki site, but has progressively moved towards a more traditional publication model, and no longer accepts either user comments or edits.

Zero Day Exploit

An attack against a software vulnerability that has not yet been addressed by the software maintainers. These attacks are difficult to defend against as they are often undisclosed by a vendor until a fix is available, leaving victims unaware of the exposure.

About the Author

John Ottman is President and CEO of Application Security, Inc., (AppSec) and has over 30 years of experience in the enterprise software industry.

Prior to joining AppSec, John was President, Global Operations at Princeton Softech, Inc., a high-growth company and leading provider of enterprise data management software which was acquired by IBM in 2007. John was also Executive Vice President of Corio, Inc. where he led the company from the startup phase, to a successful IPO and ultimately through the acquisition of Corio by IBM. Prior to Corio, John spent 10 years at Oracle Corporation in various field executive roles including Group Vice President, Industrial Sector. Before Oracle he worked at Wang Laboratories, Inc. for eight years.

About the Foreword

KENNETH A. MINIHAN,

Lieutenant General Ken Minihan retired from the US Air Force on June 1, 1999, after more than 33 years of active commissioned service to the nation. On his final tour of duty he served as the 14th Director of the National Security Agency/Central Security Service, a combat support agency of the Department of Defense with military and civilian personnel stationed worldwide. As Director, he was the senior uniformed intelligence officer in the Department of Defense. He has also served as the Director of the Defense Intelligence Agency. He has over thirty years' experience in national, defense and military information services, information technology development and diverse customer support services. Lieutenant General Minihan is a Managing Director at Paladin Capital Group and sits on the board of directors for various private and publicly traded companies. Among his awards and decorations are the National Security Medal, the Defense Distinguished Service Medal, the Bronze Star, and the National Intelligence Distinguished Service Medal.

Other Resources

- www.teamSHATTER.com
- Ponemon
- Verizon
- Northrop Grumman
- Securosis
- 451 Group
- Forrester Research
- Gartner
- Enterprise Strategy Group
- ComputerWorld
- eWeek
- Dark Reading
- Threat Post

INDEX

www.ingramcontent.com/pod-product-compliance
Lightning Source LLC
Chambersburg PA
CBHW051241050326
40689CB00007B/1026